THE MYTHOLOGY OF PLANTS

J. PAUL GETTY MUSEUM • LOS ANGELES

THE MYTHOLOGY OF PLANTS

Botanical Lore from Ancient Greece and Rome

ANNETTE GIESECKE

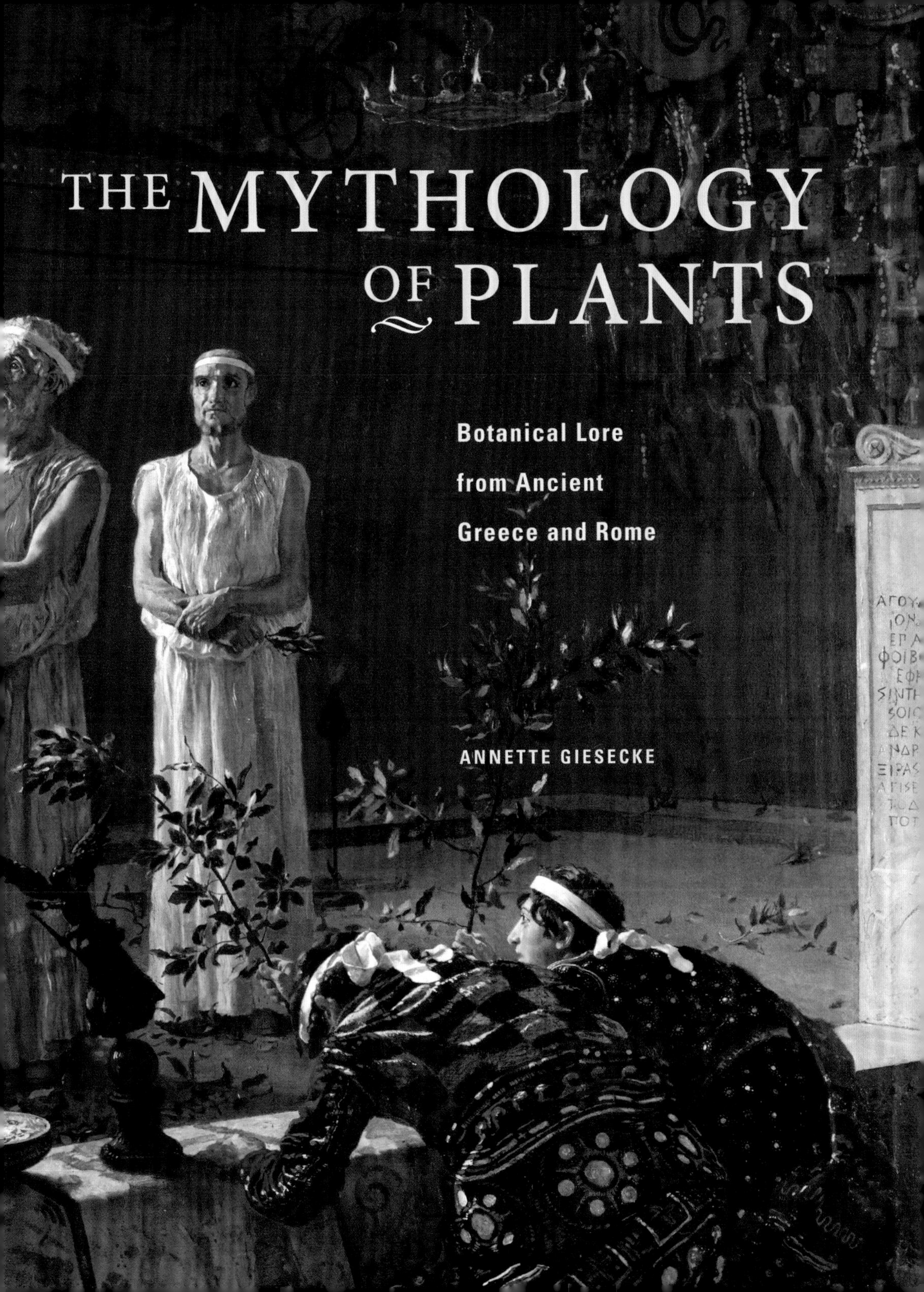

CONTENTS

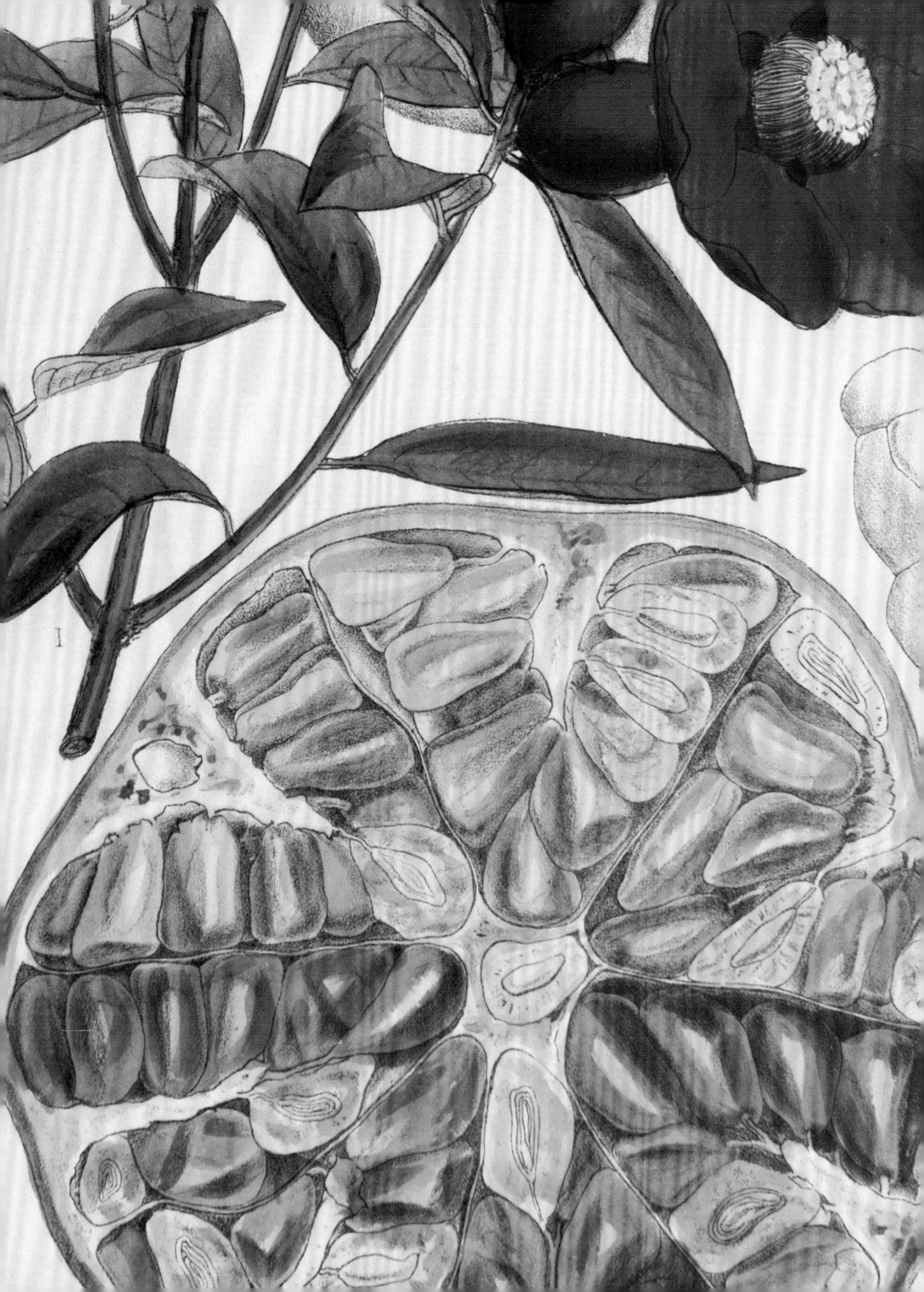
I

PREFACE

The Mythology of Plants is designed to provide enthusiasts of both mythology and the garden with a sampling of the numerous plants known and prized in ancient Greece and Rome. In those societies, all life—whether plant, animal, or human—was believed to be intimately connected with the divine; consequently the mythology of plants is a topic of enormous scope. It is curious that few books are dedicated to this subject; among those that are, even the best too often attempt to be all inclusive, listing the myths associated with various plants, but without relating the stories in any detail. This book, by contrast, limits its selection of plants to those species that feature in the *Metamorphoses*, an epic poem written by Ovid, the Roman poet who is among the finest and most celebrated storytellers of the classical world. In addition, the descriptions herein of gardens, plants, and myths are enhanced throughout by photographs of Greek painted vases, Pompeian gardens, and Roman frescoes and statuary; European paintings from the fifteenth century and later; and nineteenth-century botanical prints.

A brief introduction to the gardens, plants, and plant lore of ancient Greece and Rome provides the background necessary for appreciating the intimacy of the plant-human relationship found in classical culture. Thereupon follow the best known and most fully developed of Ovid's plant-related myths, grouped first by theme (to give some sense of the content and structure of Ovid's poem)—gods in love, hubris and human excess, piety and devotion, and mortals in love—and then by plant. Each tale is prefaced with botanical information and an account of the plant's religious, medicinal, culinary, and other uses in antiquity. In these accounts Greek names for deities and heroes have been employed in references to Greek cultural contexts and literary works, while Roman names have been adopted for references to the culture and literature of Rome. The myths themselves are new prose translations by the author, made from Ovid's original Latin texts and incorporating creative license only when a literal translation could result in misreading or confusion. Ovid's poetic style is at once dramatic and learned. His scholarly allusions, as well as his use of second-person narration—he addresses the characters directly at particularly emotional or tense times in the stories—have been preserved. Finally, the plant-associated myths that Ovid recounts briefly or mentions only in passing are grouped alphabetically by plant, without organization by theme, in the section entitled *A Guided Walk through Ovid's Garden.*

In order to assist the reader's navigation of this garden of myth, a map of the ancient Mediterranean world and a glossary, which includes the most frequently mentioned names (those of gods and of ancient authors) and relatively obscure geographic and mythological references in Ovid's poem, are provided. These are supplemented by notes identifying direct references to the writings of other ancient authors. Each book in the list of sources was consulted in the preparation of this work, and all are suitable references for readers wishing to delve more deeply into this subject.

ACKNOWLEDGMENTS

A debt of gratitude is owed to a number of individuals without whose support this book could not have taken its present form. Among them are Kenneth Lapatin, who encouraged the project from its inception; Donald Dunham, who patiently fielded myriad questions regarding organization and content; Melinda Zoehrer, who verified the text's botanical accuracy; and Daniel Lees, who generously offered expert guidance on matters of style. At Getty Publications, I am grateful to Robert T. Flynn, editor in chief, for taking the project on; Beatrice Hohenegger, project editor, for adeptly guiding the manuscript through the editorial process; Jane Bobko for her sensitive copy editing; and designer Kurt Hauser, production coordinator Elizabeth Kahn, and permissions coordinator Pam Moffat for enabling the union of text and images on which this book's identity so heavily depends. The majority of the images could not have been obtained without the assistance of Tim Murray and his staff at the University of Delaware, Morris Library, Special Collections; Lauri Perkins at the Winterthur Library, Printed Book and Periodical Collection; and the Soprintendenza Speciale per i Beni Archeologici, in Naples and Pompeii as well as Rome, all of whom allowed and facilitated extensive study and photography.

Annette Giesecke

Figure 1. Venus in the shell. Fresco from the garden of the House of Venus in the Shell (detail), Pompeii, *regio* II.3.3, after A.D. 62

INTRODUCTION

Gods and Heroes in the Garden

The Garden of Venus in the Shell

In the shadow of Vesuvius lies an extraordinary domestic garden. This botanical oasis, which contains some well-preserved garden murals, is the focal point of the ancient Pompeian house known today as the House of Venus in the Shell. For a visitor to the archaeological site of Pompeii, the house would be easy to miss were it not for a discreet sign posted on its exterior. The exteriors of ancient Roman houses were, by modern standards, remarkably restrained, and like all the other houses at Pompeii, this one does not boast of, or even hint at, the treasures within. Passing from the street into the vestibule, the visitor hasn't long to wait for the house to reveal its secret. Opposite the entry, beyond a glittering pool of collected rainwater, a mass of greenery is visible through an opening in the deep red and ocher walls of the house's atrium, or formal reception hall. This opening is the point of transition from the more public to the more private spaces of the house.

Once within the house's private zone, one is surprised to realize that the garden's plantings dominate the architecture that surrounds them—and not the other way around. The garden is not an unruly cottage garden but a precisely ordered topiary garden of deep green, clumping myrtle and yew, punctuated by dark pink roses and demarcated by squared myrtle hedges. Although the garden's original plantings are irretrievably lost, both the species and the general arrangement of the flora here are based on diverse literary and archaeological sources, and thus capture an original spirit and intent. This rectangular garden space, situated so as to be visible from every room around it, is laid out symmetrically in two beds divided by a path. As one approaches the path, a vivid mural painted on the wall at the garden's far end comes into view: in the center of the fresco, the goddess Venus reclines on an oversized conch shell that floats on a blue-green sea (fig. 1). Her cloak billowing behind her in the breeze, the goddess wears only an array of elegant golden jewels. Accompanying her are winged cupids, one riding a dolphin through the waves. This painting simultaneously represents the birth of Venus who, as the Greek poet Hesiod writes, was born from the ocean's waves, and mimics a view out to sea, such as that enjoyed by some of the grander houses in Pompeii.[1]

Venus may be the centerpiece of the mural, but other arresting scenes have been depicted here as well. On either side of the goddess are paintings representing views into densely planted gardens populated by a variety of birds (figs. 2, 3). Orioles, pigeons, titmice, swallows, thrushes, and shrikes flit through the air or settle on branches, while herons perch on the low garden fence and stride along the garden floor. Recognizable among the plantings are shrubs of oleander and myrtle in flower, rosebushes laden with red blooms, diminutive pines, and a clump of southernwood, as well as fruit-bearing strawberry trees and cherry plums. Both garden vistas are framed by a decorative garland of ivy, with a theater mask hanging from its topmost point, and both form backdrops for a piece of sculpted marble garden art. Painted in front of the garden to the goddess's right is a statue of Mars, god of war, and painted before the garden to her left is a bubbling fountain, which some of the birds use as a bath. The theater masks are emblems of Bacchus, best known as the god of wine, but also the patron of the dramatic arts—and a common presence in Roman gardens (as is discussed below).

This exceptional garden, with its rich plantings and dramatic frescoes, was clearly the heart of the house in every sense, and greatly valued. It made it possible for the owners to live immersed in nature. Filled with birdsong and the scent of roses, this tranquil spot would have provided a refuge from the shouts of beggars and hucksters, the clatter of carts, the raucous laughter of sailors, the clanging of a smithy's iron, and all the other clamor produced just outside the house's door by the inhabitants of this once-bustling port town.

Figure 2. Statue of Mars. Fresco from the garden of the House of Venus in the Shell (detail), Pompeii, *regio* II.3.3, after A.D. 62

Figure 3. Garden fountain. Fresco from the garden of the House of Venus in the Shell (detail), Pompeii, *regio* II.3.3, after A.D. 62

The Roman House and Garden

As early excavations tended to ignore or destroy gardens and garden paintings, the House of Venus in the Shell offers a unique impression of Roman domestic space. Most houses in Pompeii, however, did have gardens embedded within, many of them visible from the entry. So did the houses at Herculaneum and other ancient sites on the Bay of Naples that were buried and preserved by the eruption of Vesuvius in A.D. 79. There is a great deal of variation among individual ground plans, but such variation occurs around a core of rooms and garden areas having a more or less formulaic arrangement.

Upon crossing the threshold of a Roman town house, one walks through a constricted passageway called the *fauces*—literally, the "jaws" of the house. The *fauces* lead directly into the atrium, a light-filled public reception area at the center of which lies an impluvium, a catch basin for collecting rainwater. In oldest times the core of the Roman house, the atrium was surrounded by a series of rooms, some of them likely bedrooms, called *cubicula* by the Romans. At the far end of the atrium lies the tablinum, the homeowner's office, and beyond that lies the garden, surrounded by a colonnaded covered walkway known as a peristyle. A series of rooms for dining, relaxing, and entertaining are arranged around the peristyle. The peristyle garden is frequently more or less on an axis with the *fauces*, atrium, and tablinum, and this is the reason it is often visible from the moment of entry. This interior, open-air garden was fitted out with fountains and collections of statuary that included likenesses of animals as well as those of athletes, philosophers, gods, and various mythological characters (fig. 4). If the gardens were particularly small or lay adjacent to a wall, the planted spaces were illusionistically expanded by garden murals like those of the House of Venus in the Shell. Such garden murals were not always painted with strict botanical accuracy; instead, they often coupled an impressionistic style with the paradisiacal effect of spontaneous bloom and fruit production irrespective of seasonality. Nevertheless, garden paintings do provide some of the best evidence for the appearance of peristyle gardens and the plants they contained. Judging from these paintings, as well as from scientific evidence such as carbonized seeds and root cavities preserved by Vesuvius's pyroclastic flow, Roman domestic gardens were lushly planted with herbs, flowers, trees, and shrubs. Some of the plants were native, others imported; some were ornamental, others—the vast majority—were also edible or otherwise potentially useful.

Figure 4. Peristyle garden, House of L. Caecilius Jucundus, Pompeii, *regio* V.1.26. This house was built in the late third or early second century B.C. and was extensively remodeled in the first half of the first century A.D.

Figure 5. Peristyle garden with ornamental fishponds, Estate of Julia Felix, Pompeii, *regio* II.4.2–12. The city block occupied by this expansive estate was first inhabited in the early second century B.C., and the estate itself—some two-thirds of which was dedicated to garden spaces—continued to evolve until the eruption of Vesuvius in A.D. 79.

Although Vesuvius's eruption has preserved the impression that Roman householders lived in harmony with nature, surrounded by the sights, sounds, and scents of the gardens in their homes, this had not always been the case. As exemplified by the House of the Surgeon in Pompeii, which likely dates from the second half of the third century B.C., early Italian houses did contain gardens, but these were located to the rear of the house and were primarily what one would describe as kitchen gardens, provisioning the household. Two primary factors determined the relocation of the garden from the rear to the heart of the house—and a shift in emphasis from productive to increasingly ornamental plantings. The first of these was the integration of the peristyle into the plan of the traditional Roman house, from the late third century B.C. onward. Peristyles were not a native Italian architectural form; they were borrowed and adapted from the Greek world, where they served as a feature of public rather than domestic architecture. The Greeks, however, apparently did not plant their public peristyle courtyards, nor did they plant the small open courts at the center of their houses. Courtyards in the homes of classical Greece were additional spaces in which to work or play, but were not used as gardens. Gardens in general were utilitarian in the Greek world and took the form of orchards, vineyards, and fields of grain, as well as market gardens where fruit, vegetables, and flowers were grown. There were also sacred plantings associated with temples and tombs. Trees were planted in marketplaces and *gymnasia* (exercise grounds) to provide shade from the harsh Mediterranean sun, but there were no gardens that one could describe as being purely ornamental pleasure gardens.

The second factor that influenced the evolution of the Roman domestic garden from appendage to focal point was directly related to the first—or rather, the two went hand in hand. This was the explosion of Roman villa construction. Enriched by foreign conquests as well as by increasingly available opportunities for gain in an Italy ravaged by civil war (property was made available by proscriptions and failed agricultural reforms, and there was an ample supply of slave labor), wealthy Romans acquired a taste for sprawling villas with lavish gardens that were both productive and ornamental. Their owners filled these estates with magnificent collections of statuary, much of it created by Greek sculptors, and they commissioned lively frescoes having mythological and botanical themes to decorate their houses' walls. The estates' grounds, meanwhile, contained orchards, vineyards, and sculpture-filled formal gardens boasting elaborate fountains and pools, the latter sometimes used for swimming or

raising exotic fish (fig. 5). The grounds also featured a wide variety of architectural refinements such as towers and covered walkways from which to enjoy expansive views, as well as exercise grounds, bath complexes, aviaries, column-encircled halls, and vast chambers to store the villas' own produce. From the letters of the Roman statesman, philosopher, and author Cicero we learn that his villa incorporated a replica of the Academy, Plato's famous school of philosophy, which Cicero wanted to furnish with thematically appropriate statuary.[2] Indeed, it was standard practice to outfit one's villa with structures meant to recall a wide range of monuments or topographical features from around a world increasingly under Roman control. The Nile River, "Babylonian" hanging gardens, and Persian-style hunting parks, known as *paradeisoi* (paradises), were all reproduced, though on a scale suited to an estate setting.

Figure 6. Fresco with sanctuary garden, oecus (entertainment room) 15 of the Villa of Poppaea at Oplontis (detail), Torre Annunziata, ca. 50–40 B.C.

Such monuments, many of them having some connection with gardens, were re-created not only in built form as garden follies but also in paint, on the walls of bedrooms, dining rooms, and chambers of entertainment. Among the best-preserved paintings of this sort is an illusionistic view into a sanctuary garden that adorns a wall of a chamber in the so-called Villa of Poppaea (fig. 6). This villa, excavated from its Vesuvian burial at the ancient site of Oplontis (modern Torre Annunziata), is thought to have belonged to the family of the emperor Nero's wife. The sanctuary portrayed here is a precinct of Apollo, the god of prophecy and healing, whose sacred bronze tripod stands in the center of a leafy peristyle garden, its gate left ajar. At the neighboring site of Boscoreale a bedroom in a rustic villa was decorated with a mural depicting a sanctuary of Diana, goddess of wild places and of the hunt. In the painting, smoke still rises from an incense burner standing before the goddess's cult statue, lending the composition a mystical feel. On another wall appears a cluster of town houses, and on still another, a rustic grotto shaded by a pergola and cooled by an ornate fountain.

Important models for Roman villa design were the palaces and estates of the monarchs, governors, and officials who had inherited administration of the massive empire forged by Alexander the Great. This empire, created between 336 and 323 B.C., stretched from the Ionian Sea to the Himalaya, uniting European Greece with the territories of the Persian Empire, including Asia Minor, Syria, and Egypt. In the spirit of Alexander's desire to mingle Greek culture with the cultures of the peoples whom he conquered, these palaces and estates blended Greek, Persian, Mesopotamian, and Egyptian influences. Such amalgamation was especially evident in the great palace built in Alexandria by the Ptolemaic kings of Egypt. Covering a quarter of the city's total area, this royal complex contained not only a palace nestled amid spacious parks but also a theater, an area for wrestling and boxing (a *palaestra*), a gymnasium, and temples, as well as zoological and botanical gardens.

Roman villas were initially built as luxury retreats on the Tyrrhenian coast, from Pisa to Salerno, which offered both spectacular views and a pleasant climate. The Villa of Poppaea at Oplontis, mentioned above, and the Villa of the Papyri at Herculaneum, as well as the Villa Arianna and the Villa San Marco at Stabiae, are particularly good examples of coastal villas. Eventually, however, villas came to be built not only in the areas just outside the walls of Rome but even in the city's center, in spite of the difficulty of finding sufficient open space to construct them. Moreover, it was not uncommon for Romans with sufficient means to own more than one villa. Naturally, ownership of multiple villas brought bragging rights that could enhance one's social prestige and political clout. Indeed, the villa became an extraordinarily important symbol of one's social status, and for this reason wealthy Romans entered into a lively competition to outdo their peers in villa buying and decorating. The right choice of sculpture for one's collection—Greek masterpieces as well as busts of renowned philosophers and statesmen—could make one appear cultured and learned. Exotic landscape features would suggest that the villa's owner had symbolically achieved world dominion and was equal in stature (at least in his own home) to the great kings of Persia and Egypt, figures wealthy and powerful enough to create lush, water-filled gardens in the harshest desert climates. At the same time, though, the Romans were a people with extremely conservative values, and it was important not to stray too far from the agrarian ties of one's virtuous ancestors. Much was therefore made of the productive capacity of the Roman villa as well, which provided a potent rationale for equipping one's villas with orchards, vineyards, fisheries, oyster beds, and rabbit farms—features simultaneously extravagant and rustic.

It was not long before the villa fashion of the Roman aristocracy spilled over into the lesser Italian towns of Pompeii and Herculaneum, where householders began to transform their town houses into miniature villas. Besides the House of Venus in the Shell, described above, one such Pompeian miniature is the house next door, whose garden is easily twice the size of its interior living spaces. Known as the House of Octavius Quartio, this dwelling has not one but three garden areas. The first is the atrium, containing a flower-rimmed impluvium with a decorative fountain; the second, a small peristyle; and the third, an expansive garden, part orchard and part park, that lies beyond the peristyle. This large main garden, outfitted with vine-clad pergolas creating a shaded walk, includes elaborate water features—fountains and decorative channels recalling both the temple tombs of Egypt and the palaces of ancient Persia.

Among the statuettes that decorated this garden were representations of Egyptian-style sphinxes; animals attacking their prey; the god Bacchus; a pair of Muses, patron goddesses of the arts; and the hero Hercules as a baby, strangling a snake. In addition to statuary, paintings of a Persian-style hunting park, of Venus's birth, and of tragic themes drawn from the world of myth served to decorate this garden. Here the handsome and fatally self-absorbed Narcissus as well as the star-crossed young lovers Pyramus and Thisbe appear (fig. 7; see also fig. 43).

Figure 7. Pyramus and Thisbe. Fresco from the main garden terrace of the House of Octavius Quartio (detail), Pompeii, *regio* II.2.2, after A.D. 62

Mythology in the Garden

At first glance, it might seem that the garden art, both statuary and painting, found in the House of Venus in the Shell and in the House of Octavius Quartio was largely an eclectic mix chosen more for effect than thematic content. Even so, if sphinxes suggested the gardens of Egyptian kings, and sculpted Muses conjured the distant sanctuary gardens of Greece, what meaning appropriate to gardens did representations of gods such as Venus, Mars, and Bacchus convey? And why fill one's garden with heart-wrenching scenes from the world of myth? Closer investigation reveals that these gods and mythical personalities had strong ties with nature and plant life, and their presence enhanced the religious or paradisiacal quality of the garden. What's more, even if gods and mythological characters were not represented in garden art, so many garden plants had ties to the world of myth that the Roman garden was always filled with an otherworldly aura.

Among the gods found most frequently in Roman gardens is Venus. As the goddess of love and erotic desire, Venus was believed to be the source of fertility and life in humans, animals, and plants. Since it was through her power and favor that flowers bloomed and fruit ripened, Venus was viewed as the protector of gardens. Roman religion, like other aspects of Roman culture, was heavily influenced by the outside world, particularly by Greece, and early on Venus had become identified with the Greek goddess Aphrodite, who came equipped with an extensive mythology. Representations of the goddess's miraculous birth from the sea made for wonderful garden decor, as did fountains and other water features, which hinted at the goddess's presence. Cupid, whom the Greeks knew as Eros, was another potent god of love, represented either as the goddess's son or as a close companion. Venus's lover was Mars, an ancient Italian god of agriculture and war, who became identified with the Greek god Ares. Both Cupid and Mars, a god of love and a god of agriculture, would be natural additions to garden art, and their close ties with the goddess of gardens made them all the more appropriate. Although Venus was linked to all plant life, certain plants were particularly sacred to her. These included the rose and myrtle, both of which were associated in legend

with her birth. The most highly valued and most extensively cultivated flower in antiquity, the rose was said to have sprung from the sand, suffusing the earth with color, when Venus emerged from the waves.[3] And before the Graces came to clothe the newly born goddess in robes of divine splendor, she sought shelter behind a myrtle bush. Rose and myrtle, planted around Venus's temples and worn in garlands by her celebrants, would remain symbols of the goddess and her powers.

An even more popular fixture of the Roman garden was Bacchus, the Roman equivalent of the Greek god Dionysus, the god of wine and the vintage (fig. 8). Bacchus's presence in the garden signaled merriment and good cheer, as did the presence of the nymphs and satyrs who were his constant mythological companions. But there was more to this god and his powers than an enabling of festive pleasures. He originated as the god of liquid life—of the life-sustaining fluids in plants, in particular. Luxuriant plant growth was therefore viewed as a direct result of his influence. Over time the god also became associated with wine, milk, and honey, all fluids that were both life-sustaining and derived from nature. Worshipping this god brought tremendous benefits, for in his eyes all were equal: young and old, male and female, slave and freeman, even animal and human. Wine, considered his greatest gift to humankind, was an important source of relief from the worries and hardships of daily life; and contrary to the misconceptions of the unenlightened, this god frowned on overindulgence. One could commune with the god by drinking not only wine but also milk, honey, or the blood of animals freshly killed in an ecstatic trance. In their increasingly urban environment, the citizens of Athens found a way other than animal slaughter to honor their god. In Athens he would be honored by dramatic performances, and as this art form had been invented in his honor, he became the god of the theater. Thus the depiction of a tragic or comic mask—both highly popular subjects among mosaicists, sculptors, and painters—was enough to suggest the god's presence. The same was true of clusters of grapes and the vines upon which they grew, whether they were planted in the garden or appeared as a decorative motif on a painted wall, a mosaic pavement, or a carved garden furnishing. In addition to the grape, ivy was particularly sacred to Bacchus. An evergreen

Figure 8. Head of the young Bacchus, Roman, A.D. 1–50. Bronze and silver, H. 21.6 cm (8½ in.). Los Angeles, J. Paul Getty Museum, 96.AB.52

Figure 9. Hercules and the golden apples of the Hesperides. Fresco from the *caldarium* (hot bath chamber) of the Villa of Poppaea at Oplontis (detail), Torre Annunziata, ca. A.D. 1–15

plant, ivy symbolized eternal life and was therefore a fitting emblem of this miracle-working deity.

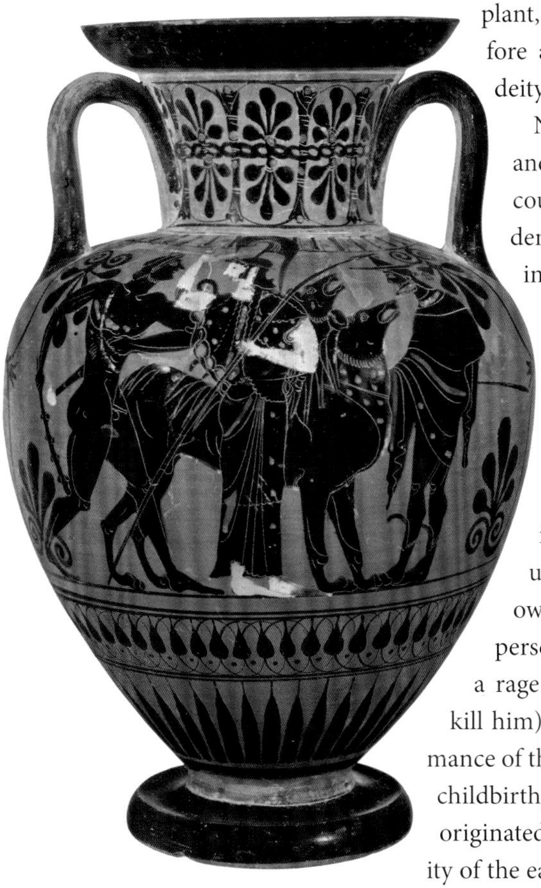

Not only gods but also a variety of heroes and heroines having ties to the plant world could regularly be found in the Roman garden—Hercules, for instance, revered for having rid the world of a host of monsters such as the dread Nemean Lion, the man-slaying Stymphalian Birds, and the grotesque Hydra of Lerna that grew new heads to replace those that were lopped off. This hero might seem slightly out of place in gardens filled with references to a life-giving Venus or to Bacchus and his celebrants until one recalls that Hercules ultimately owed his fame to the goddess Juno, whose persecution of the hero began at his birth (in a rage this queen of the gods sent a serpent to kill him). It was she who set in motion his performance of the Twelve Labors. Goddess of marriage and childbirth, Juno (known to the Greeks as Hera) likely originated as another deity responsible for the fertility of the earth. In the world of horticulture, the vitex, pomegranate, and apple were sacred to her. The apple tree and its fruit, like the pomegranate, symbolized fertility, and according to legend the earth goddess Gaia created the apple as a wedding gift for Juno. The first apple tree, which happened to bear golden apples, was tended by nymphs known as the Hesperides and guarded by a serpent. Besides slaying the monsters mentioned above, the ostensibly impossible tasks set for Hercules by Juno included fetching one of these golden apples (fig. 9; see also fig. 45); when he succeeded, the hero, too, became linked to the apple's lore. Later, Hercules was sent to capture the triple-headed dog Cerberus, who guarded the underworld (fig. 10). When Hercules dragged Cerberus up from his home beneath the earth, the dog barked and struggled furiously. As the

Figure 10. Hercules and Cerberus. Black-figure amphora (storage jar) with Dionysus and Ariadne, Greek, Athens, ca. 510 B.C. Attributed to the Leagros Group. Terracotta, H. 30.2 cm (11 7/8 in.). Los Angeles, J. Paul Getty Museum, 86.AE.80

Roman poet Ovid recounts, foam and slobber from the hellhound's mouth fell on the soil, producing monkshood, a suitably toxic plant.[4]

Many characters from myth engendered or are linked with plants. Among other well-known examples are Narcissus, who, entranced by his own reflection, wasted away to become the flower that bears his name; and Hyacinthus, fatally wounded by a discus and commemorated by a hyacinth growing from his pooling blood. The lovely Daphne became a laurel tree to escape the love-struck god Apollo's relentless pursuit, and young Pyramus, believing his beloved Thisbe dead, fell upon his sword, his spurting blood forever staining the mulberry's white fruit. These stories and others are collected in Ovid's *Metamorphoses*, the epic poem that has been the primary source of Greek and Roman mythology since the end of the first century A.D. Ovid was imitated even in his lifetime, was read and quoted in the Middle Ages, and became a favorite in the Renaissance. Over the ages countless authors and artists have incurred a debt to him, among them Chaucer, Shakespeare, Titian, Bernini, and Mozart. Plant mythology is not Ovid's sole focus, so his treatment of it is not exhaustive. Botanical myths pervade the *Metamorphoses*, however, making it a worthy selection as the source of the myths recounted in the following pages.

Ovid's *Metamorphoses* and the Mythology of Plants

Publius Ovidius Naso, known to us as Ovid (fig. 11), was born at one of the most significant moments in Roman history. The precise date of his birth was March 20, 43 B.C., just a year after the assassination of Julius Caesar. The murder of Caesar, a shrewd and far-sighted politician as well as a consummate military tactician, was momentous enough in itself. That it also provided an opportunity for Caesar's adoptive son, Octavian, to become the dominant figure in Roman politics was a consequence of immense importance. The rise of Octavian, who would come to be called Augustus, went hand in hand with the transformation of Rome from a republic governed by both elected officials and the body of elite citizens making up the Senate to an empire controlled by a single individual. This was a radical though perhaps inevitable shift, as Rome had by then extended her territory far beyond the shores of Italy. Rome's old constitution, perfectly suitable for a relatively small, conservatively minded agrarian community, had become obsolete. However unavoidable constitutional change may have been, it was also the case that Romans had a deep-seated suspicion of any protracted concentration of power in the hands of one person; this was, after all, what had occasioned the untimely death of Caesar. The first de facto emperor in a country intolerant of monarchy, Octavian had to tread with care. He capitalized on his having put an end to decades of civil war so intense and bloody that it threatened irreparably to rend Roman society, and promoted himself as author of a new era of universal peace. Under the auspices of Rome's First Citizen, as Octavian styled himself, the republican constitution was restored, at least in name, as a new age of harmony and plenty, founded on piety and the agrarian values of old, commenced.

It was, accordingly, an era of peace and stability in which Ovid came of age; it was also what has come to be known as the golden age of Roman literary production. Ovid's education had not been geared

toward preparing him for a literary career—his family envisioned a life of politics for him—but the writing of poetry seems to have become a full-time occupation for Ovid when he was in his twenties. Witty, urbane, learned, and focused largely on matters of the heart, his early poetic endeavors met with approbation and acclaim, reflecting as they did a mood different from the lofty, often somber or moralizing tones of Vergil and Horace, older contemporaries who had witnessed the horrors of civil war and the heavy price of the ensuing Augustan peace. But Ovid proved to be too free a spirit for the regime under which he lived. In A.D. 8, the emperor ordered Ovid's exile to Tomi, a city on the shore of the Black Sea, at the easternmost fringes of the Roman Empire—in Roman eyes, the edge of the civilized world. In Ovid's own words, this unwelcome development was the result of "a poem and a mistake" (*carmen et error*).[5] Lively debate about Ovid's reference continues, but the poem and error may be one and the same, namely the work entitled *The Art of Love*. Devoted to the art of seduction and glorifying adultery, this poem appeared to mock much that Augustus and his regime officially stood for: family values, piety, and the production of legitimate offspring. Thus Ovid would spend his last years in what he describes, with distaste, as an inhospitable, even savage cultural wasteland.

The *Metamorphoses*, the poetic tour de force for which Ovid is chiefly known, is thought to have been substantially complete when he left for Tomi. Indeed, it is fortunate that it survived, given that its author reports angrily consigning it ("still taking shape and rough," in his words) to flames prior to his exile.[6] In both form and content, the *Metamorphoses* was unprecedented. The work was divided into fifteen parts, signaling that it was an epic poem different from Homer's and Vergil's texts, which were divided into an even number of books or chapters. Nor was Ovid's subject matter that of his predecessors: the heroic deeds of a superhuman figure such as the warrior Achilles or Aeneas, originator of the future Roman state, do not dominate the narrative here. Instead, the reader encounters a vast, seemingly eclectic assemblage of Greek and Roman myths tenuously united only by the motif of transformation, generally of a human or divine being into an animal or plant.

Figure 11. Luigi Ademollo (Italian, 1764–1849), frontispiece for *P. Ovidii Nasonis Metamorphoseon Libri XV cum Appositis Italico Carmine Interpretationibus ac Notis* (Florence, 1824; repr. 1832), vol. 1. The Phoenician princess Europa, abducted by Jupiter (disguised as a white bull), holds aloft a medal inscribed with Ovid's name and likeness.

The sheer number of collected myths, as well as their vivid poetic treatment, secured for all posterity Ovid's distinction as chief Greco-Roman mythographer. But as one would expect of a poet with Ovid's talent, the *Metamorphoses* is more than a repository of tales myriad and colorful. The reader's first impression of the work as an expression of tumultuous spontaneity is quickly disproved upon closer inspection. Indeed, the multiplicity of devices accounting for the poem's intricate architecture provides the stories with an inherent cohesion. Apart from the fact that most of the myths recounted entail a change of form, the overarching narrative progression is chronological, commencing at the beginning of time, with the birth of the known world, and culminating in the deification of Julius Caesar.

Within this temporal frame, three primary story divisions have been recognized: a first group concentrating on gods and their interactions with humans, a second on human actors, and a third on historical and quasi-historical figures. Embedded in these groupings, which have broad thematic connections with each other, are smaller clusters—myths closely related in theme, setting, or the family ties of the protagonists. Thus, for example, the story of the self-absorbed youth Narcissus shares the theme of hubris with the story of Pentheus, a young prince of Thebes who refused to acknowledge the divinity of Bacchus, his own cousin. Narcissus would become the flower that bears his name, and Pentheus, the victim of a primal sacrifice to the god he disdained. The tale of Pentheus, in particular, is one of a group of narratives that have to do with members of the royal house of Thebes; another is the tale of the princess Europa: she was abducted and raped by Jupiter, who had transformed himself into an irresistibly lovely, tame white bull. What emerges from Ovid's treatment of the assembled myths is a picture of both gods and humans that is less than flattering; their actions are governed by blinding lust, greed, and vengeance more often than magnanimity and foresight. While the power of the gods is absolute, their dispensation of justice is often quite unjust. The guilty can count on being punished, but blamelessness and piety are no guarantee of divine reward. The only constant in Ovid's universe is mutability: the earth and all its creatures—even the gods above—are eternally subject to unpredictable change.

I

Gods in Love

1
2
3
4
5
6
7
8
9
10

Bay Laurel LAURUS NOBILIS

The mythological associations of the bay laurel (figs. 12, 13), known also by the common names of sweet bay, bay tree, and Grecian laurel, made it one of the most culturally significant plants in ancient Greece and Rome. Native to the Mediterranean region, this broad-leaved evergreen can take the form of a large shrub or relatively small tree, reaching heights of eight to twelve meters (26–40 ft.). Its bushy growth habit and small leaves make it an ideal plant for trimming into hedges or topiary. In spring the laurel's glossy leaves are offset by yellow-green flowers that, on female plants, are followed by black berries. While certainly popular in antiquity as an ornamental garden plant, the laurel was also used in cooking and for medicinal purposes. Its aromatic leaves could enhance the flavor of meats or stews, and whether soaked or pressed to extract their potent oil, were believed to cure a host of illnesses ranging from general exhaustion to influenza and disorders of the liver and kidneys.

In the mythological realm, the laurel was sacred to Apollo, god of music, archery, healing, and prophetic utterances. Appropriately, a famous laurel tree grew at the god's primary sanctuary of Delphi, which lies on the slopes of Mount Parnassus in Greece; and according to the Greek travel writer Pausanias, Apollo's first temple on the site was constructed entirely of laurel.[1] Thought to be the center of the earth, Delphi was the location of the most important oracle in the classical world. It was this oracle that forewarned Oedipus that he would one day kill his father and marry his mother. It was this same oracle that predicted the overthrow of the wealthy Lydian king Croesus by the Persians and that prophesied the future greatness of Alexander the Great. Those consulting the oracle posed their questions to the

Figure 12. David Blair (Scottish, 1852–1925), *Laurus nobilis, Linn.* From Robert Bentley and Henry Trimen, *Medicinal Plants. . . .* (London, 1880), vol. 3, no. 221

Figure 13. Wreath with detached stem including leaves and detached berries, Greek, B.C. 300–100. Gold, 26.3 (front to back) × 34 (side to side) cm (10⅜ × 13⅜ in.). Los Angeles, J. Paul Getty Museum, 92.AM.89. Gold wreaths such as this—delicate and costly replicas of wreaths made of real laurel branches—were dedicated as gifts to the gods or served as honorific funerary offerings.

Pythia, Apollo's priestess, who reportedly inhaled intoxicating vapors arising from a fissure in the earth and chewed laurel leaves to enhance her psychic trance (fig. 14).

Various myths relate the manner in which the laurel became sacred to Apollo. Best known is the story told by Ovid in which Apollo fell desperately in love with Daphne, the daughter of the river god Peneus. Although Daphne did not return Apollo's affection, he pursued her relentlessly. It is this story that explains both the Greek name *daphne* for the laurel and Apollo's motivation for designating this tree as his sacred emblem. Other sources link the laurel directly to the god's acquisition of the oracle at Delphi, which had not always belonged to him. According to the Roman author Aelian, Delphi was first sacred to the earth goddess Gaia, whose monstrous son, the serpent Python, guarded the oracle.[2] Apollo slew Python, and having gone to the nearby valley of Tempe to wash off the serpent's blood, he returned victoriously to Delphi wearing a crown made of the laurel that grew

abundantly throughout the valley. Thus the laurel became a symbol of victory possessing an inherent purifying potency. In Greece, crowns of laurel were given to victors at the Pythian Games, athletic contests held at Delphi in honor of Apollo. Additionally, laurel branches were used to sweep holy places, to purify houses polluted by death, and to safeguard supplicants.

As was the case with much of Greek culture, the laurel and its symbolism carried over into Rome. Here the laurel wreath not only symbolized victory but also served as an emblem of distinction and a signifier of peace, prosperity, and healing. In the Roman world the primary means of achieving prominence was through military conquest, and Roman generals celebrating their triumphs wore crowns of laurel and carried laurel branches in their hands. One such victorious general was Augustus, who attributed his success in avenging Caesar's murder and in establishing an era of peace and prosperity after years of civil war to the protection of Apollo. As a result, Apollo

Figure 14. Camillo Miola (Italian, 1840–1919), *The Oracle*, 1880. Oil on canvas, 108 × 142.9 cm (42½ × 56¼ in.). Los Angeles, J. Paul Getty Museum, 72.PA.32

and his symbols, the laurel among them, appeared everywhere in the art, architecture, and general cultural fabric of Augustan Rome. Two laurel trees flanked the entrance of Augustus's house, purposefully located next to the Temple of Apollo on Rome's Palatine Hill.

The laurel's symbolism of peace, abundance, healing, and victory guaranteed this plant a place of prominence in two of the most extraordinary extant examples of Augustan art. One is the famous paradisiacal garden mural that decorated the walls of a subterranean dining room in the villa at Prima Porta belonging to the emperor's wife, Livia (see pp. 31, 57, 91, 101, 115), and the other is the vegetal scroll that decorates the Altar of Peace (Ara Pacis), erected by Augustus as a monument to an anticipated eternal end to war.

OVID DAPHNE AND APOLLO

Met. 1.452–567

Daphne, Peneus's daughter, was Apollo's first love—a love born not of blind fate but rather of Cupid's savage anger. The god of Delos, full of pride at his victory over the serpent, had recently caught sight of Cupid flexing a bow, its string pulled tautly back, and said, "What do you want, impudent boy, with powerful weapons? Those armaments of yours are more suitable for my shoulders, as my aim is true when seeking to wound beasts or a hostile foe. It is I who just a short while ago laid low the rage-swollen Python with myriad arrows so that now its noxious belly presses heavily on a vast tract of land. Be content to ignite whatever loves you want with your torch, but lay no claim to the source of my glory."

To him the son of Venus made answer: "Better your bow strike everything else, Phoebus Apollo, but let mine strike you. And however much all living things are inferior to a god, so much lesser is your glory than mine."

Thus he spoke and tore forcefully through the air with beating wings, alighting on the shady summit of Parnassus. Two arrows he drew from out his quiver, each for a different purpose: the one to drive love away, the other to cause it. The one for love gleams golden from its sharp tip. The other is muted with lead within its shaft. At the daughter of

Peneus he shot this last, while with the first he wounded Apollo to the very marrow, right through the bone. Straightaway was Apollo filled with love, while Daphne, now shunning the very idea of a lover, instead rejoiced in the forest's haunts and the prize of animals taken captive, as she, a ribbon binding her unruly locks, strove to emulate Diana, Apollo's maiden sister. Many men sought her hand, but spurning her suitors, she wandered instead through the pathless forests. Unfettered by a husband, she cared not at all for marriage or love or wedded life.

Yet often her father said, "My daughter, you owe me a son-in-law." Often he said, "My child, you owe me grandchildren." But her abhorrence of the marriage ceremony as if it were a mortal crime sent a modest blush over her lovely cheeks. Then clinging to her father's neck, hoping to persuade him, she pleaded, "Dearest Father, let me enjoy the benefits of virginity forever! This a father once granted to Diana." He, for his part, was persuaded, yet that beauty of yours, Daphne, prohibited what you desired. Your loveliness opposed your vow.

Once laying eyes on Daphne, Phoebus was in love and wanted to marry her. What he desired, he hoped would actually happen, ignoring his own oracles. As thin stalks of grain are burned when the heads have been cut and as hedges are set ablaze by the torch of a traveler who, by chance, has come too close or has dropped it at the arrival of dawn, so the god burst into flames. So did his whole heart burn, as he fed his unrequited love with hope. Gazing at the unadorned locks hanging loose at her neck, he wondered aloud, "How might they look if combed?" He beheld her eyes, shining like stars. He beheld her lips. But looking was not enough. Praise he showered on her fingers and hands and forearms and arms bared nearly to the shoulder. If any part of her was hidden, he imagined it better still. Yet she, meanwhile, fled more swiftly than a light breeze, nor did she pause as Apollo called to her: "Nymph, daughter of Peneus, wait! Not with hostile intent do I pursue you. Wait, nymph! So does a ewe flee the wolf, so a doe the lion, so, too, fearful doves the eagle, for each tries to escape her own enemies. But the cause for my pursuit is love! Oh, poor me! May you not fall, may thorns not mar those legs that should suffer no such indignity. The terrain over which you run is rough. I beg you, run more slowly, and hold back somewhat in your flight; I myself will pursue with more restraint. Yet ask, at very least, who it is whose fancy you have captured. No mountain dweller I, no herdsman. I am not some unkempt rustic who watches over flocks and herds. You know not, rash one—simply do not know—who it is you flee and for that reason flee me. Delphi, Claros, Tenedos, and the kingdom of Patara—all are subject to me. Jupiter himself is my father, and through my agency, future, past, and present are all revealed. Through my power, songs harmonize with the lyre. True is my arrow's aim, yet another's, admittedly, was aimed more truly still. How deeply it wounded my erstwhile carefree heart. Medicine is my invention, and through all the world I am known as the one who brings relief. The healing potency of herbs is subject to me. Oh, how unlucky for me that no herbs can cure the ill of love and that those arts of mine, available for the help of all others, are denied to me!

More still he would have said, but in fear the daughter of Peneus fled. Both him and his unfinished words she left behind. Even then she was lovely to behold, her body's shape revealed by strong winds as she ran through gusts that made her garments flutter, a breeze blowing back her hair. In truth, her beauty was enhanced in flight. And since the youthful god could endure to waste his flattery no longer, compelled by love itself, he followed in her footsteps with unchecked stride. As when a Gallic hound has spied a hare in an open field, the one relies on fleet feet to reach his prey, the other to seek safety—the one, now almost close enough to grasp with his teeth, trying again and again to seize his prey and grazing the hare's heels with his extended snout. His prey, uncertain whether caught, bolts from reach of those deadly jaws and lips that just were touching. So it was with the god and the maiden—he made swift by hope and she by fear. But helped in his pursuit by wings of love, he was swifter and denied her any rest. She fled headlong, and looming just behind, he breathed upon the hair flowing down her neck. Her strength completely spent, she grew pale. Overcome by flight's exertion, she cried, "Open your jaws, oh Earth, and annihilate those looks of mine that cause me such injury"—then looking toward Peneus's waves, said, "Help me, Father! If you have a river's divine power, change and corrupt these looks that have drawn too much attention."

Scarcely did she finish her prayer when a heavy sluggishness overtook her limbs, and her soft chest became enclosed by bark. Her hair grew

into leaves, her arms into branches. Her foot, but recently so swift, clung heavily to the earth with roots unyielding, and her face was supplanted by a treetop (fig. 15). Her radiance alone remained intact. Yet even like this Phoebus loved her, and touching the trunk with his right hand, felt her heart still trembling beneath the freshly grown bark. Embracing the branches as if a body still, he planted a kiss upon the wood, but the wood shrank before his kiss. "Though you cannot be my wife," spoke the god to her, "you will be my sacred tree. My hair will always be adorned with your leaves, sweet laurel, as will my cithara and quiver. You will accompany the commanders of Latium, a joyous voice singing 'Triumph!' as the Capitoline beholds long processions of victory. Most trusted sentinel, you will stand guard at the approach to Augustus's door and will behold the entrance's wreath of oak. And just as uncut locks adorn my youthful head, you, too, shall wear the eternal honor of your leaves!" So ended Apollo's speech; and to this the laurel signaled assent with her freshly grown branches, seeming to nod her crown.

Figure 15. Jan Boekhorst (Flemish, born Germany, ca. 1604–1668), *Daphne and Apollo*, ca. 1640. Black chalk, pen and brown ink, watercolor, and white gouache heightening, 22.5 × 23.2 cm (8⅞ × 9⅛ in.). Los Angeles, J. Paul Getty Museum, 2003.112

1
2
3
4
5
6
7
8
9

Pomegranate PUNICA GRANATUM

Taking the form of an upright deciduous shrub or small rounded tree (5–8 m, or 16–26 ft.), the pomegranate (figs. 16, 17) is native to Persia (modern Iran). It was well known in Greece at least by the eighth century B.C., when Homer depicts it in the *Odyssey* as planted in the paradisiacal orchards of the mythical, island-dwelling Phaiakians.[3] An attractive ornamental specimen as well as a productive plant, the pomegranate has glossy, bright green leaves, and over the summer months bears striking orange-red flowers. These flowers are followed by fruit of thick, red rind containing a multitude of seeds—from several hundred to over a thousand—encased in iridescent red flesh.

Pomegranate seeds were eaten fresh, alone or as an accompaniment for other foods. For instance, a character in the novel *Satyricon*, by the Roman author Petronius, serves a dish of sausages accompanied by plums and pomegranate seeds.[4] Pomegranate seeds were also pressed to yield juice that could be used in the production of pomegranate wine. But not only the seeds of the pomegranate were considered useful in antiquity. In his *Natural History*, Pliny the Elder lists a great variety of medicinal and practical household applications for which virtually every part of the plant was employed.[5] Pomegranate flowers, having astringent qualities, were used to prevent the spreading of sores; to remedy the sting of scorpions; to cure dysentery; and, mixed with wine and vulture's lungs, to stop the spitting up of blood. Pomegranate rind could be burnt to deter gnats, or ground to serve as an ingredient in perfumes and in a host of medicines, the latter either applied topically or ingested. These were used in the treatment of ailments ranging from the relatively minor, such as earaches, bruises, indigestion, and morning sickness, to the severe,

Figure 16. David Blair (Scottish, 1852–1925), *Punica granatum, Linn.* From Robert Bentley and Henry Trimen, *Medicinal Plants. . . .* (London, 1880), vol. 2, no. 113

such as paralysis, gangrene, and epilepsy. According to Pliny, the pomegranate's rind was also utilized in the curing of leather. He also made the (somewhat baffling) claim that the pomegranate's branches "have the effect of repelling the attacks of serpents."

Perhaps most interesting are observations made by the Greek physician Soranus regarding the contraceptive agency of pomegranate rind when applied in the form of a poultice or suppository.[6] Such a theory is directly linked to the pomegranate's numerous seeds and blood-red juice, which together underlie its important function in myth and religion as a potent symbol of fertility and life. As such, the pomegranate appeared in representations of Aphrodite, the divine incarnation of sexuality and desire, as well as of Hera, goddess of marriage and childbirth. Even Apollo, god of the sun's life-giving warmth, and Hermes, who also had a connection with fertility, were associated with the pomegranate.

Although a symbol of life, the pomegranate was also linked with death and the afterlife, themes vividly illustrated in the tale of Persephone's abduction. Persephone, or Proserpina, was the daughter of Ceres, goddess of grain and the harvest (and known to the

Figure 17. Aryballos (perfume container) in the shape of a pomegranate, Greek (Corinthian), early 6th century B.C. Terracotta, H. 7.8 cm (3 1/16 in.). Los Angeles, J. Paul Getty Museum, 78.AE.349. This vessel was suitable for everyday use, but because of the pomegranate's association with Persephone and the underworld, it was also a particularly appropriate funerary offering, perhaps embodying hopes for a felicitous afterlife.

Greeks as Demeter). While picking flowers in a Sicilian woodland, Persephone was spotted by Hades (called also Dis and Pluto), god of the underworld. Instantly smitten, he desired her as his bride. It was a pomegranate's fruit that consigned Persephone to a life divided between the world of the living and the kingdom of Hades, where she was the god's unwilling queen. During Persephone's months in the underworld, Ceres would remain in mourning, thereby preventing crops from growing. Persephone thus represents the seed corn that, when sown in autumn, descends into the earth only to reemerge, transformed into verdant shoots at the coming of spring.

OVID PLUTO AND PERSEPHONE

Met. 5.385–571

Not far from Enna's city walls is a lake of deep water, Pergus by name. Even on the river Cayster's flowing currents are not more swans' songs to be heard. A woodland encircles its waters, girding its full length and protecting it from Phoebus's rays with its foliage. Dense branches provide a coolness, and the moist soil yields variegated flowers. Perpetually it is spring. Here in this grove Proserpina amused herself, picking violets and lilies gleaming white. Trying to outdo her friends in picking, filling her baskets and her tunic's hanging folds with the enthusiasm of a child, she was spotted by Dis, desired by him, and snatched away by force—so sudden was love's onset (fig. 18). Terrified, the goddess in sorrowful tones called out to both her mother and her companions, most often to her mother. Distraught, she ripped her garment, tearing it down from the neck. From the discarded tunic fell those gathered flowers. Such was the innocence of her young years that these spilled flowers became a further cause for sorrow. Her abductor urged his chariot onward, calling his horses by name, slapping ominous, dark-dyed reins on their necks and manes. Through the deep lakes and the Palici's sulfur-smelling pools, bubbling up from cracks in the earth, he drove, and drove, too, by the place where the Bacchidae, a family to be born at Corinth, that city situated between two seas, would build their new city walls between unequal harbors.

Between neighboring springs, Cyane and Pisaean Arethusa, there is a bay whose waters narrow, confined by jutting points of land. Here lived the nymph Cyane, from whom the spring received its name, of all Sicilian nymphs most honored. Rising up from the water's midst as far as her waist, she recognized the goddess Proserpina. "Your journey soon will end," Cyane said to Pluto, "for you cannot be Ceres's son-in-law against her will. The maiden should have been sought in marriage properly, not seized by force! And if I may compare lesser events with this one, Anapis took a fancy to me, yet courted me and married me, unlike this girl, without terror." So she spoke and stretching her arms out wide, blocked his path. The god, Saturn's son, did not check his anger: he urged on his dread horses and with his mighty arm hurled the royal scepter into the pool's depths, burying it there. The earth,

Figure 18. Alessandro Allori (Italian, 1535–1607), *The Abduction of Proserpine*, 1570. Oil on panel, 228.6 × 348 cm (90 × 137 in.). Los Angeles, J. Paul Getty Museum, 73.PB.73

when struck, opened a passage to Tartarus and received the chariot, plunging headlong into the opening's center.

Cyane lamented the rape of the goddess and the disrespect shown her pool. Speechlessly she nursed the inconsolable wound, and consumed by her own tears, dissolved to blend with those very waters whose great protector she had once been. You could have watched her limbs grow limp, her bones bend, her nails lose their stiffness, and the liquefaction of her sky-blue locks, her frail toes and fingers, her ankles, and her feet: for delicate parts the transition to icy water is swift. Next her shoulders, back, side, and breast faded into the clear cold stream. At last water took the place of living blood in her weakened veins, and nothing that you could have touched remained.

Meanwhile, the fearful mother searched for her daughter in vain over all the earth and the depths of the sea. Neither the arrival of Aurora, her hair wet with dew, nor that of Hesperus found her resting; lighting two branches of pine with Etna's fires, she carried them ceaselessly through the frosty darkness. Then again, when the life-giving light of day had blunted the stars, she would seek her daughter from the direction of the sun's setting to that of its rising. . . .

What lands and seas the goddess wandered through would be long to tell—the whole of earth did not suffice to end her search. Traversing all regions on her journey, she returned to Sicily, seeking Cyane. Had the nymph not been transformed, she would have told Ceres everything—though willing, Cyane had neither mouth nor tongue, nor any means by which to speak. She revealed Persephone's girdle, well known to her mother, floating in the water, which, by chance, had fallen off there in the sacred pool. Recognizing it and realizing that her daughter had been stolen, the goddess tore at her disheveled hair and with her hands beat her chest repeatedly. Still not grasping where her daughter was, she reproached all lands of the earth, calling them ungrateful, undeserving of her gift of crops, particularly Sicily, where she had come upon the traces of her great loss. And so there with savage hand, she shattered the plows that turn the soil and, filled with anger, joined both farmers and the pasture-dwelling cattle equally in death. She ordered the very fields to default on what was invested in them, causing the seed to spoil. The reputation of the country for fertility, known in all quarters of the globe, was now a lie, in ruins. As they sent up their first shoots, the crops died. Sometimes excessive heat, sometimes excessive rain destroyed them. Both stars and winds brought ill effects, and greedy birds consumed the seed that had been sown. Darnel and thorny caltrop, and also stubborn grasses, plagued the harvests of wheat.

Arethusa, nymph loved by Alpheus, then raised her head from the currents of her Eleian spring, and pushing her wet hair away from her brow to her ears, said, "Oh you who have sought your daughter over all the earth and who are the mother of all crops, cease from your prodigious toils and do not, in violence, grow angry at a land loyal to you. This land deserved no punishment and only countenanced the rape all-unwilling. Yet I am not a supplicant on behalf of homeland: I have come here as a guest. Pisa was my land of birth, and my waters sprung from Elis. I live in Sicily as a foreigner, but this land is more pleasing to me than any other. It is here I keep my household gods; it is this place I call my home. May you, most gentle one, preserve it! Just why I moved, borne to Ortygia across the waters of such vast seas, I can tell you in a more suitable time, when you are unburdened from worry and have a kindlier demeanor. The permeable earth provided me passage, and flowing down beneath the caverns of the nether regions, I raised my head here and beheld most unfamiliar stars. Well, as I glided beneath the earth on the eddy of the river Styx, I with my own eyes saw Proserpina there. Sad she was, indeed, fear still written on her face. But she was a queen and most exalted in all the world of darkness, powerful consort of the Infernal Lord.

The mother was stunned at these words, as if turned to stone, and long remained like someone stricken speechless. But soon deep paralysis was displaced by deep anger, and she departed in her chariot to the realms of heaven. There she stood before Jove, her whole face clouded in worry, an indecorous sight with her unkempt hair. "I have come to you as a supplicant, Jupiter," she pleaded, "on behalf of my child and yours. If I, the mother, hold no favor, may his daughter move her father. I pray you, let not your concern for her be diminished because she was born from my womb. Long sought, at last she was found by me—if learning of her certain loss, or knowing where she is, means finding her. Her abduction I will tolerate, so long as he returns her! Even if she were not my daughter but only yours, she surely does not deserve a thief as husband.

"Our daughter," Jupiter responded, "is a shared pledge and a worry for both me and you. If you want to assign right words to things, this was not done by way of malice, rather of love. Nor is that son-in-law a source of shame, if only you were willing to see this. Never mind everything else—how great is it to be Jove's brother! What for the fact that he lacks nothing except what he lost to me by fate? If you so desire the dissolution of this union, Proserpina may return to the heavens, though under this certain caveat: that no food has crossed her lips there in the lower world, for thus it is decreed by the law of the Fates."

So he spoke, convincing Ceres that she might retrieve her daughter. But the Fates did not allow it, as the maiden had indeed broken her fast: while wandering alone in the well-tended gardens, she'd plucked a ruby fruit, a pomegranate, from a bending tree, and taking seven seeds from its pale rind, she pressed them in her mouth. Only one witnessed that: Ascalaphus, born in the gloomy woods to Orphne (not least known among Avernus's nymphs) and the river god Acheron in the gloomy woods. Yes, he saw it and cruelly prevented her return by informing on her. At this the Queen of Erebus cried out and swiftly changed that accursed witness into a bird. . . .

Jupiter, however, mediating between his brother and his sorrowing sister, divided the year's course equally. Now the goddess Proserpina, a potent deity in both realms, would spend an equal number of months with her mother and husband. Straightaway her appearance—her thought, her mien—changed, and she, whom even Dis saw as sad, bore an expression of joy, just as the sun bursts victorious through obscuring clouds.

V

Hyacinth HYACINTHUS ORIENTALIS, OR OTHER FLOWERS

Although a common garden plant bears the name "hyacinth," the flower for which Ovid uses the name is among the most difficult of all the plants in his *Metamorphoses* to identify botanically. According to Ovid, the deep purple hyacinth sprang from the blood of the god Apollo's favorite, the handsome Spartan youth Hyacinthus, fatally injured by a recoiling discus. This flower would eternally memorialize Apollo's grief over the passing of the youth, its petals bearing the Greek words of lamentation "Ai, ai." Apollo himself took the title "Hyacinthius," and the Spartans instituted an annual festival in the young man's honor. Other ancient authors add that the hyacinth is spring flowering and sweet smelling and has arching leaves.[7]

The most natural candidate for Ovid's flower is the oriental hyacinth, *Hyacinthus orientalis* (fig. 19), which is native to southern and central Turkey, northwestern Syria, and Lebanon. A bulbous perennial, the oriental hyacinth has lance-shaped leaves and produces spikes bearing up to forty very fragrant purple flowers in early spring. This flower does not, however, appear to bear the words "Ai, ai," and herein lies the source of much debate over the identity of Ovid's flower. Among the flowers proposed as Ovid's true hyacinth are several varieties of wild orchid and the corn lily, a wild gladiolus of Greece and Turkey (*Gladiolus illyricus*) that is purple flowering and has distinctive marks on its lower lip.

The fragrant hyacinth described in ancient sources was an important ingredient in the making of perfumes and the fabrication of garlands. Its strong scent, both soporific and sensual, made it a natural element in tales of seduction. So, for instance, the hyacinth is one of the flowers among which the goddess Hera famously seduces Zeus in Homer's *Iliad*.[8] With Zeus thus distracted, the Greeks gain the upper hand in their ten-year battle with the Trojans.

Figure 19. Maria Sibylla Merian (German, 1647–1717), *Hyacinth* (*Hyacinthus orientalis*). From *De Europische insecten* (Amsterdam, 1730), fig. V, GRI.89-B10813

OVID APOLLO AND HYACINTHUS

Met. 10.162–219

You, too, Hyacinthus, Apollo would have placed in the realms of heaven if the sad Fates had allowed time enough. Though to some degree you are immortal still; as often as spring has repelled the winter frosts and Aries succeeded rainy Pisces, so often do you sprout and flower in the green turf.

The god Apollo loved you beyond all others. Delphi, center of the world, was without its presiding deity while he frequented the river Eurotas and Sparta, the city lacking walls. He showed no regard for his cithara or arrows. Utterly forgetful of his true self, he disdained not to carry hunting nets, to hold on to dogs, to accompany the youth walking along the ridges of a rugged mountain, and so fed love's flame through protracted intimacy. Now the sun was about midway between night's arrival and its passing, equally far from both: the god and youth removed the clothing from their bodies, and gleaming with olive oil, began to compete at the broad discus. Apollo first balanced it and then hurled the discus high into the air, its weight dispersing the clouds in its path. Long airborne, cast by skill joined with strength, the massive object at last fell to the hard ground. Straightaway, incautious and eager to make his own throw, the Spartan youth hastened to retrieve the disk, but the solid ground caused it to rebound, striking your face, Hyacinthus. The god grew pale—as did the boy—catching at the youth's sinking limbs. Now he tried to revive you, tending your lamentable wounds, staying the escape of your life's breath by applying herbs. His skills proved useless; the wound could not be healed. Just as when in a well-watered garden one plucks violets and poppies and lilies bristling with yellow pistils, these of a sudden lower their drooping heads, unable to hold themselves upright, their tops facing the ground. So, too, was your face downcast in death, your strength gone, your neck upon your shoulder, too heavy for itself (fig. 20).

"Oh, scion of Oebalus, you slip away, defrauded of your early youth," cried Phoebus Apollo. "I behold your wounds, my wrongdoing. You are the source of my grief and the essence of my crime. My right hand should be branded for your death. It is I who am the author of your

passing. Yet what exactly is my crime? Can suffering for love or love be called a crime? If only I could restore your life for you! Alas, I am constrained by the laws of death. But you will always be with me and linger on my unforgetting lips. My songs and the lyre, strummed by my hands, will remember you, who taking the form of a new flower will reproduce my lamentations in its markings. The time will come when Ajax, that strongest of heroes, will associate himself with this flower, his name to be read on the petals."

While such truly spoken words left Apollo's lips—behold!—the blood that had flowed upon the earth, staining the grass, ceased to be blood. Up sprang a purple flower, brighter even than Phoenician dye, having the appearance of a lily but without a silvery white. For Apollo this did not suffice (he was the artist of this honor), and inscribing his lamentations on its petals, caused the flower to read "Ai, ai," the cries of mourning. Nor is Sparta ashamed of having produced Hyacinthus; his honor endures to the present day, and in the manner of their ancestors, the city's folk must annually celebrate the Festival of Hyacinthus, displaying the year's fresh growth.

Figure 20. Giovanni Battista Tiepolo (Italian, 1696–1770), *The Death of Hyacinthus*, ca. 1752–53. Oil on canvas, 287 × 232 cm (113 × 91 5/16 in.). Madrid, Museo Thyssen-Bornemisza

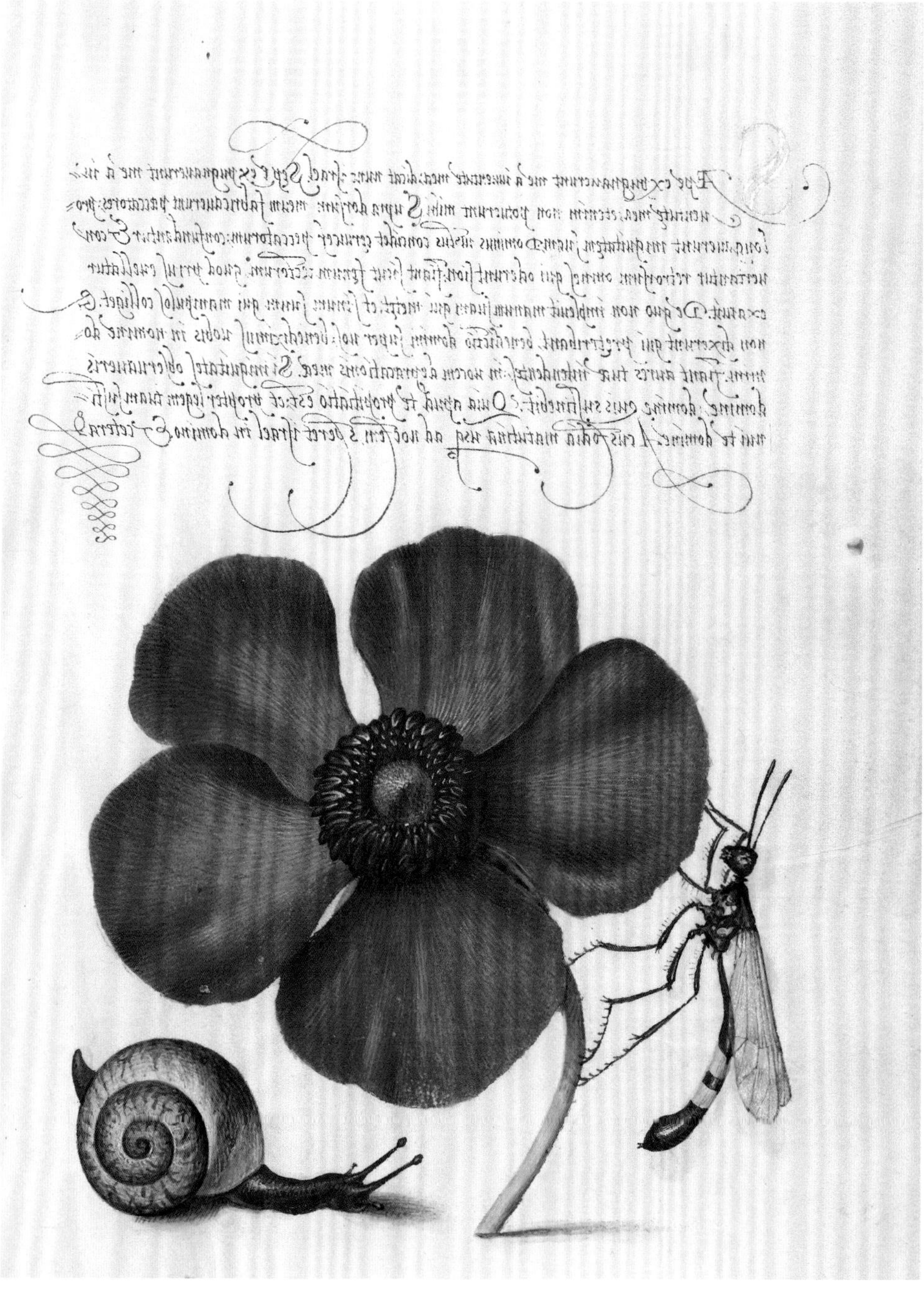

Poppy Anemone ANEMONE CORONARIA

The poppy anemone (fig. 21), or Greek windflower, is among the most typical and showy wildflowers of Greece and the Mediterranean. Found equally on rocky hillsides, in olive groves, and in vineyards, in spring the poppy anemone produces a single brilliant red, lavender, or white flower on a tall stem with a whorl of small leaves just below the flower. As sources such as the Roman naturalist Pliny the Elder report, the flower never opens, except while the wind is blowing, which is the source of the name "windflower" (*anemone* in Greek).[9]

The Greek botanist Dioscorides records a range of medicinal uses of the anemone's root.[10] When poured into the nostrils, its juice purges the head, and when chewed, the root serves to dislodge phlegm. Soaked in wine, the root cures inflammations and other afflictions of the eyes. The anemone's leaves and stalks were key ingredients in concoctions used to counteract the stoppage of milk in women and promote the menstrual discharge. Pliny the Elder adds that those skilled in the arts of magic recommended the anemone to dispel fevers.[11] The plant's hygienic efficacy, however, depended on gathering the flower as soon as it appeared, uttering certain words while gathering it, and keeping it in the shade, wrapped in a red cloth, so that it might readily be attached to an afflicted person upon the onset of symptoms.

In the realm of myth and religion, the anemone is closely associated with the tragic tale of Venus and the handsome youth Adonis. Grazed by one of Cupid's arrows, Venus became so enamored of Adonis that she abandoned her comfortable sanctuaries to accompany him in the harsh wilderness where he went to hunt. To no avail, she warned him of hunting's dangers: the hunter might, quite by accident, slay a beast sacred to the gods, thus committing a punishable sacrilege—and might himself become the hunted.

Figure 21. Joris Hoefnagel (Flemish/Hungarian, 1542–1600), *Terrestrial Mollusk, Poppy Anemone, and Crane Fly,* 1591–96. From Georg Bocskay, *Mira Calligraphiae Monumenta* (Vienna, 1561–62), Ms. 20, fol. 66. Watercolors, gold and silver paint, and ink on parchment, 16.6 × 12.4 cm (6 9/16 × 4 7/8 in.). Los Angeles, J. Paul Getty Museum, 86.MV.527.66. The calligraphic text is an example of mirror script, written in reverse.

Although according to myth Adonis was the product of Myrrha's incestuous love—and was a mortal—the Greeks venerated him as a god and celebrated him at a festival called the Adonia (see the discussion of myrrh in chapter II). In the course of this two-day festival, the passing of Adonis was mourned and his resurrection celebrated by the planting of Adonis gardens. Women carried these small gardens (pots or baskets planted with seeds of grain and vegetables) to rooftops and terraces. There seedlings would quickly sprout, and just as quickly wither, occasioning a renewal of ritualized grief. The anthropological meaning of the Adonis-garden tradition has long been a matter of discussion and debate; at its core it appears to be an ancient form of seed testing.

OVID VENUS AND ADONIS

Met. 10.519–739

Fleeting time slipped by unnoticed, for nothing is swifter than passing years. Adonis, a child born of his own sister and grandfather, had only just been hidden deep within a tree (his mother's womb!). The babe soon became a handsome youth and then a man more handsome still. Before long he caught the eye of Venus, thus avenging his mother Myrrha's ill-placed passion; for while young Cupid, a quiver on his shoulder, had been kissing his divine mother, he accidentally grazed her breast with the exposed tip of an arrow. Thus wounded, the goddess pushed aside her son, but the cut, deceiving even her, was deeper than it looked.

And so, enthralled by Adonis's beauty, she no longer cared for Cythera's shores nor returned to seagirt Paphos or Cnidus, a city rich in fish, or Amathus, a place abounding in metals. She even stayed away from the heavens. To heaven Adonis was preferred. To him did she hold fast, to him alone become companion. Though accustomed always to enjoy the shade and to enhance her beauty by assiduous grooming, she now ranged the forests and brush-covered crags. Like the huntress Diana with gown raised to the knee, she urged on the dogs in pursuit of the safest prey: darting hares, stately-antlered bucks, and does. From boars, ravening wolves, and sharp-clawed bears she kept her distance—so, too, from lions glutted with the slaughter of cattle

Figure 22. Hans Bol (Flemish, 1534–1593), *Landscape with the Story of Venus and Adonis*, 1589. Gouache heightened with gold on parchment, 20.6 × 25.7 cm (8⅛ × 10⅛ in.). Los Angeles, J. Paul Getty Museum, 92.GG.28

Figure 23 (detail of fig. 22). The scene shows the metamorphosis of Adonis into the anemone.

(fig. 22). You as well, Adonis, did she admonish to fear such beasts, saying in the hope that this might do some good, "Before those that flee be bold." But adding: "Bravery cannot be safe in the face of bravery. Refrain from rashness, oh youth, lest you endanger me, nor provoke those beasts that nature has armed lest your glory come at great cost to me. Neither that tender youth of yours nor that fair visage that won the heart of Venus will move lions or bristle-bearing boars or the eyes and hearts of savage beasts. Wild boars' curved tusks strike with lightning speed, and tawny lions attack with vigor and incalculable fury. . . ."

These were the warnings she issued, and she departed through the ether in a chariot drawn by swans. But manly virtue was incompatible with such warnings. It chanced that Adonis's dogs, having followed unmistakable tracks, flushed a boar from its place of concealment, and Cinyras's young son had soon hit it with an indirect cast as it made to leave the forest. Straightaway the savage boar, shaking out the bloodstained spear from its wide flank, pursued him as he ran for safety. The beast, sinking all its teeth into the youth's side, caused him to fall dying on the golden sand. Meanwhile, the goddess Cytherea, carried on swans' wings through the ether in her light chariot, was still on her way to Cyprus when from a distance she discerned his dying moans. She steered her white birds back whence she had come, and spotting his lifeless form lying in a pool of his own blood from the airy heights, she leapt down to the ground. Tearing her robe and hair and beating her chest with recriminating blows, she cried to the Fates, "Think not that everything is under your control. Memorials of my grief for you, Adonis, will remain for all time, and an annual evocation of your death will body forth a simulation of my sorrow. As for the blood that was shed, that will be transformed into a flower. Why, Persephone, if you could change a woman's limbs into fragrant mint, should not the transformation of the hero, Cinyras's son, be granted to me?" With these words, she sprinkled a perfumed nectar on the blood, which swelled up upon contact like translucent bubbles rising in a tawny sky. Not yet an hour later, a flower bloomed there, the very color of blood and like the flowers borne by the pomegranate that conceals its seeds beneath a tough rind (fig. 23). Yet enjoyment of the bloom is but brief, for the flower is ephemeral and, owing to its delicacy, prone to collapse through being shaken by the very winds that give it its name.

II

Hubris and Human Excess

Narcissus Poeticus   Narcisse des Poëtes

Narcissus NARCISSUS POETICUS, NARCISSUS SPP.

Of the fifty or so species of narcissus, it is generally the so-called poet's narcissus, *Narcissus poeticus* (fig. 24), that is identified with the narcissus that the Greeks and Romans write about. Its white flower, set off by a yellow, red-edged corolla, emerges from a single stem in spring. Other species, however, were certainly known, likely including *Narcissus serotinus*, a small autumn-flowering narcissus with narrow petals that give the flower a starlike appearance; the spring-blooming Lent lily, or *Narcissus pseudonarcissus*, with a pronounced yellow trumpet and cream perianths; and the so-called bunch-flowered narcissus, *Narcissus tazetta*, which carries up to twenty sweetly scented flowers on a single stem. Also called paperwhite, the *Narcissus tazetta* flowers between December and March.

Prized for its distinctive fragrance, the narcissus was popular in the making of perfume as well as of floral crowns and garlands, purposes for which it was grown in market gardens. It was also valued in cosmetics: in his poem *On the Art of Beauty*, Ovid lists narcissus bulbs—along with barley, vetch, eggs, and stag horns—as a necessary ingredient in the production of exfoliants.[1]

Both the botanist Dioscorides and the naturalist Pliny the Elder mention the importance of the narcissus in a range of medical applications.[2] Its roots, beaten and mixed with honey, were applied topically to extract thorns and splinters and to treat burns, bruises, abscesses, strained muscles, and painful joints. Narcissus oil was employed to soften the skin as well as to alleviate frostbite, and, if used in suppositories, to dissolve uterine tumors. The flowers, roots, and bulbs of narcissus could serve as an emetic, though they were potentially injurious to the stomach if ingested in abundance. Nevertheless,

Figure 24. Pierre Joseph Redouté (French, born Flanders, 1759–1840), *Narcissus poeticus*. From *Les liliacées* (Paris, 1801–16), vol. 3 (1807), pl. 160

the narcissus found a place in cuisine. The Roman gourmet Apicius praises the narcissus bulb as a luxury food and aphrodisiac (though his narcissus may be what is now identified as a different plant genus, the grape hyacinth, or *Muscari*), recommending that it be fried and served with sauce, or boiled and steeped in a mixture of spices, honey, vinegar, dates, and oil, topped with a dash of pepper.[3]

For all the health-promoting qualities of the narcissus, there is perhaps no other plant in the realm of classical myth and religion that is more closely associated with the gods of the underworld and death. This is vividly illustrated in the story of the abduction of Persephone, the goddess of the harvest's young daughter. According to the so-called Homeric hymn composed in the goddess's honor, the earth put forth a narcissus with one hundred blooms to lure the unsuspecting Persephone.[4] Astonished by the flowers' beauty and intoxicating fragrance, the girl reached out to pick them. At that moment, the earth gaped wide open, revealing Hades, the underworld's dark lord, who seized her. Thereafter, it was a pomegranate that, as discussed in chapter I, sealed her fate as his bride. (See also the discussions in chapter V of barley, the Madonna lily, and the violet.)

Another tale related to this flower is Ovid's tragic story of the nymph Echo—her only means of speech was an echo of someone else's words—and her passion for Narcissus, a youth so handsome that young women and young men alike desired him.

OVID ECHO AND NARCISSUS

Met. 3.351–510

Narcissus, Cephisus's son, had now reached sixteen years of age and had the appearance at once of man and boy. Many youths desired him, also many girls. Yet so great was the haughtiness attending his tender years that no youths or girls moved him.

While he was chasing skittish deer into hunters' nets, a nymph spotted him—a chatty being, who had learned neither to be silent while another talked nor to herself initiate speech. This was reverberating Echo, then still a corporeal being and not yet completely a voice. She possessed only that use of her voice she has now, namely to repeat the last words of any number that were spoken. The goddess Juno, Saturn's daughter, was the cause of this: she might have caught the nymphs who so often lay on the mountains in her husband Jupiter's embrace had it not been for clever Echo's detaining her in lengthy conversation so that the offending nymphs could flee. Once Juno caught on, she warned, "Trifling will be the power of that tongue of yours by which I have been tricked—the duration of your speech only brief." She supported her threats with action. . . .

When Echo saw Narcissus wandering through the pathless woods, she, suddenly smitten, followed him secretly. The more she followed, the more deeply did love's flame burn, the same as combustible sulfur, when smeared on the tops of torches, ignites as flames are brought near. Oh, how often she wanted to approach him with flattering words and impassioned requests! But her altered state prevented it, not allowing her even to begin. But what her new state did allow she prepared to do: wait for sounds to which she might respond.

Narcissus, by chance separated from his faithful companions, wondered aloud, "Someone is here?" "Someone is here," responded Echo. He stopped transfixed, and casting his gaze in every direction, loudly shouted, "Then come!" And she, in turn, mimicked the caller. He, looking back and seeing no one, asked, "Why do you flee from me?" In response he received only so many words as he had uttered. Gulled by the illusion of another voice, he persisted, entreating, "Let us meet here." Never more glad to respond to a sound, Echo answered: "Let us meet." Eager to act on her own words, she left the forest so that she might throw her yearning arms around his neck. Repelled, Narcissus fled: "Remove your hands; break this embrace! I would prefer to die than allow that I fall into your hands." Her only response: "Allow that I fall into your hands." Hiding in the woods, spurned and ashamed, Echo covered her face with leaves. From that time on, she inhabited only caves. Yet her love persevered, fed on the pain of refusal. Consuming worries wasted away her pitiable body. Thinness drew her flesh closer to the bone, her body's moisture dissipating into the air. All that remained were her bones and voice—then only the voice. People say that her bones took on the shape of rocks. Now she hides in the woods and is not seen on any mountain. But she is heard by all: the only thing alive in her is sound.

So it was that Narcissus had dallied with her—as with other nymphs born from the sea or mountains. So also he'd shunned relations with men. Thus one of his rejected admirers, raising hands to heaven, said: "Let him experience the same sort of love as I: let him not possess the object of his desire!" To these prayers did the goddess Nemesis assent.

There was a clear pool, silvery with glittering ripples, that neither herdsmen nor goats pastured on the mountains nor any other herd had touched. Nor had any bird or beast from the wild or any fallen branch disturbed it. All around grew grass, fed by the ready source of moisture, and a woodland that shaded the place, cooling it from the hot sun. Here the youth, drawn by the look of the place and by the pool, wearied from hunting and heat, sunk down. But when he tried to slake his thirst, another thirst grew: as he drank, he was captivated by the handsome

Figure 25. Fresco with Narcissus, House of Marcus Lucretius Fronto, Pompeii, *regio* V.4.a, ca. A.D. 40–50

face he saw (fig. 25). Mistaking water for substance, he fed his desire with incorporeal hope. Stunned by the image of himself, he became frozen, transfixed with an expression like a statue of Parian marble. Still stretched on the ground, he saw twin stars—his own eyes—and locks of hair befitting Bacchus and also Apollo, and beardless cheeks, an ivory neck, a lovely face, just a tint of rose mingled with a snowy pallor. He admired everything for which he himself had been admired. Unwittingly, he longed for himself; he who found favor was himself the favored. While he courted, he was himself courted, burning with desire. How often did he give futile kisses to that deceiving pool! How often did he, submerging his arms, grasp at the neck he saw, full into the water's midst but failing to seize himself therein! He did not know what he was looking at; but he yearned for what he saw. The very source of his deception confused him. Gullible one, why did you grasp at a fleeting image? That love you sought was nothing; you were bound to lose what you desired—you should just have turned away! What you saw was but a reflected image, a shadow. It was nothing in and of itself; it came and lingered with you. It would have left with you, if leave you could!

No concern for food, no concern for sleep could move him from the spot. Prostrate in the dark grass, he gazed insatiable upon the deceitful image. He languished through his very eyes, and rising slightly, his arms reaching for the surrounding trees, asked: "Alas, you woods, has anyone loved more cruelly? You know the answer, having provided chance concealments for many lovers. In the centuries that you have existed, can you remember anyone who has wasted away like this? I can see the object of my delight; but what I see and delight in, I nevertheless cannot possess. So great is the deception. I suffer all the more since it is no vast sea, or road, or mountain, or wall with portals locked that keeps us separate. Blocked by a paltry bit of water! He, the object of my desire, wishes to be embraced! For as often as I reached down my lips to the clear water, so often did he strain to meet me with an upturned face. One would think he could be touched—so insubstantial is that which stands in the lovers' way. Whoever you are, come out here! Why, sublime boy, do you elude me? Where do you go when I reach for you? Surely it is not my appearance or my age that drives you to flight; even nymphs have desired me. Your friendly look offers me some sort of hope. When I reach out my arms for you, you reach out in turn. When I laugh, you laugh back. Often have I noticed your tears when I was crying; nodding in response to me, you give a sign, and guessing from the movement of your lovely face, you are uttering words that do not reach my ears. Oh! But it is I myself who am what I've been calling 'you'! Now I know, nor does my reflection deceive me any longer. I burn with love for my own self: I ignite love's flames as well as suffer them. What am I to do? Should I be courted or do the courting? But why should I even court? What I long for is with me: my very wealth has made me resourceless. Oh, if only I could leave my body! My wish as a lover is without precedent: I wish that my beloved were departed! Grief

Figure 26. Nicolas Poussin (French, 1594–1665), *Echo and Narcissus*, ca. 1628–30. Oil on canvas, 74 x 100 cm (29 ⅛ × 39 ⅜ in.). Paris, Musée du Louvre

now saps my strength, nor is there much time left for me, my vital force extinguished in my prime. Death is no concern to me, as I will be rid of my cares in death; but as for him who is the object of my affection, I wish he could live on. Now we two will be joined in a single death."

Such were the words he spoke. Distraught, he turned again to that same face and disturbed the waters with his tears, his reflection now obscured by the rippled water. Seeing it dissolve, he shouted: "Where are you fleeing? Stay, and do not, oh cruel one, desert me, who loves you! If only it were possible to behold that which I cannot touch and thus obtain some solace for my frenzied sorrow!" While he grieved, he tore open his robe from its top edge and beat his bared chest with marble-white palms. Being struck, his chest assumed a rosy glow, the same as when apples, light at first in color, grow red in part, or a grape, not yet ripe, spreads a purple hue through its multicolored clusters. As the waters cleared again, he saw this plainly and could bear it no longer.

As golden wax melts with a gentle flame and morning frosts soften in the warming sun, thus did Narcissus melt, wasted away through love and consumed by hidden fire. Neither natural coloring (his pallor mixed with red) nor his force and strength—all that moments earlier had been pleasing to the beholder—nor his body, which Echo once had loved, remained. Though angry and mindful of her former hurt, seeing him she yet grieved for him, and as often as the youth cried "Alas!" she repeated the resonant cry: "Alas!" And when he struck his arms with his own hands, she repeated this sound of lamentation, too. His final words, as he looked into those familiar waters, "Woe, youth, who has been loved in vain," reverberated in the place; and when he said "Farewell," Echo, too, said her farewell (fig. 26). As he lowered his weary head in the green grass, death closed his eyes, even then admiring their owner. Even when he had been received into the netherworld, he still gazed at himself in Styx's water. His sisters, the naiad nymphs, wept over him and made offerings of their shorn locks. The dryad nymphs wept, and Echo repeated their weeping. And now they prepared a pyre, flaming torches, and a bier. But his body was nowhere. In its place they found a flower, white petals circling a saffron-yellow center.

6
1
2
3
12
4
5
6
8
10
9
11

Grape VITIS VINIFERA, AND *Ivy* HEDERA HELIX

It would be difficult to overstate the importance of the grape (fig. 27) and its products to ancient Greece and Rome. As fresh or dried fruit, and as a source of juice, wine, and vinegar, the grape was a major component of the diet and had tremendous economic and cultural value. Both the grape and wine were famously synonymous with the god Dionysus (who was originally assumed from the Near East by the Greeks and was identified by the Romans as Bacchus), and stories surrounding Dionysus shed much light on the grape's significance and history.

No single ancient text provides more information about Dionysus than the play *The Bacchae* (405 B.C.), written by the Greek tragedian Euripides. In this play the prophet Teiresias urges Pentheus, the young regent of the city of Thebes, to accept Dionysus as a god, stating that in all Greece two deities are of utmost importance: Demeter, mother earth and goddess of the harvest, who sustains humanity, and Dionysus, bringer of wine, which provides humanity relief from suffering and pain, and which, as an offering to the gods, secures for humanity all good things.[5] Dionysus is, in fact, the god not only of wine but of all life-sustaining fluids. More properly, the god is this liquid. Yet he has a dark side that Pentheus, the unbeliever, tragically experiences firsthand; ritual communion with the god can be achieved not only by drinking wine but also by partaking of blood obtained from small animals, torn apart and eaten raw.

Figure 27. David Blair (Scottish, 1852–1925), *Vitis vinifera*. From Robert Bentley and Henry Trimen, *Medicinal Plants. . . .* (London, 1880), vol. 1, no. 66

The grape is native to southern Europe and the Near East; corroborating Euripides's tale, cultivation of the vine is thought to have begun in the Caucasus region, spreading from there to Mesopotamia and Syria, among other places, and thence to Greece and Italy. In turn the Romans spread viticulture to western parts of their empire, including

France, Germany, and Hungary, making grapes, along with olives and grain, one of the three main products of Mediterranean agriculture. The grapevine is a woody, deciduous climber (fig. 28). Losing its leaves and withering in the winter, the vine appears to die, only to come dramatically back to life in spring, perhaps explaining the grapevine's deep-rooted association with the cycle of death and rebirth. Additionally, red wine, produced by fermentation of grape juice together with the fruit's skin, readily became a symbol of life in its close resemblance to blood.

Ancient sources have preserved a wealth of information about the propagation of grapevines and the making of various wine products, as have some ancient artifacts. Particularly detailed sources include the Roman authors Cato, Varro, Columella, and Pliny the Elder. From them we learn, for instance, that vines were grown supported by living trees (the elm, ash, and poplar were the most suited) as well as by stakes and trellises made from the limbs of trees such as chestnut, or from stalks of the giant reed, *Arundo donax*. We learn, too, that vines were grown—and wine produced—both on a small scale by landholders for their own consumption and on a large scale for domestic sale and export. As is the case today, not all wine was equal, due in part to the variety of grape used and differences in growing conditions. The elder Pliny knew of some ninety-one varieties of wine; among the finest were those from the Greek islands of Thasos, Chios, and Lesbos, and from the region of Italy known as Campania.[6] Both Greeks and Romans had a propensity for flavoring wine, a tendency doubtless based to some extent on the desire to mask an inferior vintage. Favorite additives included honey and herbs such as marjoram, gentian, valerian, hazelwort, rue, and thyme. Even leaves and sprigs from shrubs such as juniper and myrtle were used as flavorings, as were flower petals, primarily of the rose, and exotic incense such as frankincense and myrrh.

The chief product of viticulture, wine, together with its by-products, was consumed at all levels of society and on all occasions, religious and secular, in the home, at public venues, and in taverns. In ancient Greece, wine spawned a distinctive cultural institution, the symposium, or "drinking together," a gathering of men from the

upper classes that took place after the evening meal and provided an opportunity for all manner of discussion. The only women present were the flute girls and hetairai, the Greek equivalent of geisha, who provided entertainment. In the Roman world the symposium was replaced by the convivium, which was more inclusive and more properly a full banquet. Wine was drunk diluted with water at ratios of 1:3, 2:3, or 3:5, as determined by the symposiarch (symposium leader) or his Roman equivalent, the *magister bibendi*. Drinking undiluted wine was deemed characteristic of barbarians, and drunkenness frowned upon. A tendency toward overindulgence made some of the classical world's most renowned figures, including Alexander the Great and Mark Antony, easy targets for their political enemies.

Wine-based or wine-related products included other beverages as well as a wide array of salves and medicines. Roman authors mention a drink of twice-crushed grapes mixed with water, *lora*, that might be served to one's slaves, as well as *posca*, a mixture of sour wine and water supplied to soldiers in the Roman army. Vinegar, produced by a secondary fermentation of wine, was a culinary ingredient as well as a preservative for staple foods and herbs such as green olives, capers, parsley, and fennel. The Greek botanist Dioscorides lists an expansive array of medicinal uses of both wine and vinegar in his famous herbal, which has survived in its Latin version, *De materia medica* (The materials of medicine).[7] To cite just a few examples, vinegar mixed with brine was thought to be a remedy for ulcers and the bites of dogs or other wild beasts; squill vinegar was held to be a cure for ailments ranging from epilepsy and sciatica to loose teeth and depression; pitch wine was taken for coughs and asthma; absinthe

Figure 28. Kalathos (cup) with relief decoration, Roman, 50–1 B.C. Terracotta, H. 9.6 cm (3¾ in.). Los Angeles, J. Paul Getty Museum, 96.AE.209. A grapevine heavy with bunches of grapes sprouts from the handle of this ceramic vessel and wraps around its surface.

Hedera Helix.

wine was taken to aid digestion and diseases of the liver; and hellebore wine served as an abortive.

Figure 29. *Hedera helix*. From William Curtis, *Flora Londinensis: Containing a History of the Plants Indigenous to Great Britain*. . . . (London, 1820), vol. 3, pl. 341

Figure 30. Mask of a satyr wreathed with a garland of ivy leaves, Sikeliote (Sicilian Greek), 3rd–2nd century B.C. Terracotta with polychromy, 12 × 15.5 cm (4¾ × 6⅛ in.). Los Angeles, J. Paul Getty Museum, 96.AD.305

Another plant besides the grapevine has close associations with the god Dionysus, and that is ivy (fig. 29). A climbing plant like the grape, ivy is a vigorous perennial native to Europe, western Asia, and North Africa and is characterized by glossy dark-green leaves. Clusters of tiny flowers emerging in autumn are followed by berries.

Ivy is also evergreen, retaining its leaves in spite of the harshness of winter, and this, together with the plant's burgeoning growth habit, is key to its symbolism. The plant became a powerful symbol of life, and was even viewed as an embodiment of Dionysus himself. Where ivy grew in abundance, the god's presence was strongly felt. Such is the case with the house of Dionysus's mortal mother, Semele, in the city of Thebes, which the Greek travel writer and geographer Pausanias saw in ruins, covered with ivy.[8] An avid fan of Dionysus and of Greek culture generally, Alexander the Great was reportedly thrilled to find ivy growing in profusion in a location as remote as India. When depicted in art or described in ancient literary sources, Dionysus and his worshippers wear wreaths of ivy on their heads (fig. 30) and hold the magical thyrsus, a fennel staff having a clump of ivy at its top.

Visually attractive and deeply sacred, ivy was a favorite plant in the Roman garden. Garden paintings frequently portray ivy, often in the form of topiary mounds. In one of the statesman Cicero's letters, he memorably praises the skill of his brother's gardener, or *topiarius*, who has trained ivy to cover not only the foundations of his villa but also the columns running along the garden walk—so artfully as to create the illusion that the garden statues are this fine landscape's gardeners, proudly displaying their creations.[9] But ivy did not only decorate the surfaces on which it grew; it could also be harvested for use in making garlands to decorate the home.

Both ivy and the grape feature prominently in Ovid's tale of Dionysus's capture by pirates, itself a sequel to the story of the god's miraculous birth. As mentioned above, Dionysus (or Bacchus, as Ovid calls him) was the son of the Theban princess Semele, who had been impregnated by Zeus, appearing to her in disguise. Unsure whether the father of her unborn child was truly a god and not some imposter, Semele—her doubts fueled by a jealous Hera—asked Zeus for a favor, which he granted: Zeus revealed himself to Semele in his full divine splendor, a splendor so intense that she caught fire. Unable to save the girl, Zeus did manage to save the fetus, placing it in his thigh for incubation. Upon Dionysus's birth, he was taken to the island of Crete to be raised; when he had matured, he set off by boat to mainland Greece and Mount Olympus, the home of his father and the other gods. It was in the course of this journey that Dionysus was taken captive by pirates hoping for a generous ransom. Instead, they received their just deserts. These events, both wondrous and terrifying, are narrated by the pirate ship's captain, the only man to realize that it was a god and not some mortal prince whom his crew held in custody.

OVID BACCHUS AND THE PIRATES

Met. 3.597–691

While on the way to Delos, I, captain of that pirate ship, happened to put in on the coast of Chios, and conveyed to shore by dexterous rowing, I leapt lightly onto the wet sand. When night had passed, I rose at dawn's first blush and ordered fresh water to be brought, showing the way to the spring. I myself looked out from the top of a hill to see what the breeze might promise, and then calling to my comrades, made for the ship.

"Here we are," said Opheltes, the foremost of my crew, leading along the shore a prize—or so he thought—found in an empty field: a boy with a maiden's form. The lad appeared to stagger, heavy with wine and sleep, and to follow along with difficulty. I looked at his clothing, his appearance, his gait, and saw nothing there that could be considered mortal. This was my feeling, and I said to my companions: "What divine power resides in that body, I do not know; some otherworldly force does inhabit it. Whoever you are, be favorable toward us and assist our undertakings. Show kindness to these men, too." But Dictys, quickest at climbing to the top of the yardarm and, rope in hand, sliding down again, said, "Don't pray on our behalf." Libys agreed with this, as did the fair-haired Melanthus, watchman at the prow, and Alcimedon, and Epopeus, who called out both rest and rhythm for the oarsmen, guiding their efforts, and all the rest as well, so blind was their desire for plunder. "But I will not allow this barge of pine to be defiled by carrying a sacred freight," I answered. "The greatest authority resides with me." And I blocked their boarding.

Lycabus, boldest of the group, was furious. Exiled from an Etruscan city as punishment for a frightful killing, he punched my throat with a young man's strength while I was standing there and would have pushed me off into the water had I not clung fast, thoroughly rattled but holding to a rope. That godless crew approved what was done. At last, Bacchus (for it was *Bacchus)—as if his torpor had been dissipated and sensation restored to his body by the commotion—asked, "What are you doing? What's all the shouting? Tell me, sailors, how did I get here? Where are you preparing to take me?" "Don't be afraid," said*

Proreus. "Tell us what ports you wish to reach: you will stand on those longed-for shores." "Change your course to Naxos!" said the god. "That is my home, and it will hospitably receive you."

Deceitfully, they swore by the sea and by all the gods that it would be so and ordered me to set our brightly painted ship to sail. Naxos was on the right, and as I raised the right sail, each fearing for himself said, "What are you doing, you fool? What madness has struck you, Acoetus? Turn to the left!" Most signified their wishes with a nod, the rest with a whisper in my ear. I was astonished and said, "Let someone else be captain!" and distanced myself from taking the lead in this crime and deception. All berated me, the whole crew muttering. From among them Aethalion demanded, "Our collective safety was placed in your hands alone, was it?" Himself now assuming my position, he fulfilled

my job and headed off in a different direction, Naxos left behind.

Then the god, mocking them, as if having only now sensed their deceit, looked out to sea from the curved stern. Feigning great distress, he said, "These are not the shores you promised, sailors. Nor is this the land I requested. What did I do to deserve this punishment? What glory can there be for you, a band of men in your prime, to collude in the deceit of one, and that a mere boy?"

For some time I had been in tears, but the impious crew, laughing at our anguish, thrust forward on the water with hastening oars. I swear by his very name (for there was no god more manifestly present) that I am telling you things true even as they seem incredible: the ship stood still on the water, no differently than if a dry dock held it. Amazed, the men persisted in their rowing, and furling the sails, redoubled their efforts. Now ivy stayed the oars, creeping along with winding shoots and embellishing the sails with heavy clusters of berries. The god himself, his head crowned with branching grapes, brandished a spear draped with vine leaves. Around him crouched phantoms of tigers and lynxes and ferocious spotted panthers. One by one the men jumped overboard, whether in a fit of madness or out of fear. Medon first began to grow dark in color, bending with a pronounced curve to his spine. Lycabus began to ask, "What strange thing are you turning into?" but as he spoke these very words, Medon assumed a wide grin, a snubbed nose, and skin roughened by scales. As for Libys, as he tried to wrest free the resisting oars, he saw his hands shrink down—this in the briefest moment—so as then not to be hands but rather what could instead be called wings. Another man, wanting to reach for the braided ropes, had no arms and leapt into the waves, his limbless body bent backward and sickle-shaped tail curved like a waning moon's horns. On all sides they dove into the waves, wetting everything with spray. Then they would reappear and again return beneath the water. Cavorting like a chorus, they tossed about their bodies and blew water from their spouts (fig. 31). Of the twenty sailors—for this was the number the barge carried—I alone remained, terrified and chilled, with body trembling, scarcely in control. The god then spoke to me: "Shake fear from your heart and make straight for Naxos." Once there, I, too, joined the sacred rites and participate still in Bacchus's worship.

Figure 31. Black-figure kylix (drinking cup) with Dionysus, Greek, Athens, ca. 530 B.C. Signed by Exekias. Terracotta, DIAM. 30.5 cm (12 in.). Munich, Antikensammlungen. Dionysus-Bacchus sails in a ship among dolphins—the transformed pirates.

1
2
3
4
9
8
7
6
5

Olive OLEA EUROPAEA

One of the most important cultivated plants in classical antiquity was the olive (fig. 32), both economically and from a religious or cultural perspective. A foundation plant of Mediterranean horticulture, the olive is believed to have been domesticated in Syria and to have moved to Crete, where it was grown before 2,000 B.C., and thence to mainland Greece. From Greece, cultivation of the olive spread to Italy, and subsequently to all parts of the Roman Empire where it could flourish.

Characterized by a gnarled trunk and distinctive gray-green leaves, the olive is an evergreen shrub or tree typically not exceeding a height of fifteen meters (49 ft.). Deep-rooted and slow to mature, it produces fruit only after some five or even fifteen years, depending on the cultivar. The olive is also extraordinarily long-lived, specimens having reached ages ranging from several hundred to more than a thousand years. It was particularly devastating, therefore, when the Spartans and their allies destroyed Athenian olive groves in the course of the long war that, at the end of the fifth century B.C., would bring the golden age of Athenian political and cultural dominance to its end.

Although the olive's most valuable product was the oil yielded by its fruit, virtually every part of this plant was used in antiquity. Olive wood found applications in construction and carving, where it was selected in the fabrication of items such as doorjambs and statuary. Olive leaves, discovered to possess astringent as well as detergent properties, were employed to treat a variety of medical conditions, including ulcers, headaches, and afflictions of the eyes. The fruit of the olive was cured in brine and consumed, or, of course, pressed in the production of oil. A versatile product, olive oil was burned as fuel in oil lamps, utilized as a moisturizer for the skin, and employed as

Figure 32. David Blair (Scottish, 1852–1925), *Olea europaea, L.* From Robert Bentley and Henry Trimen, *Medicinal Plants. . . .* (London, 1880), vol. 3, no. 172

a cleanser, first applied to the body and then scraped off. The Greek travel writer Pausanias recounts that olive oil was a preservative for ivory; the enormous gold-and-ivory statue of Zeus at Olympia, he observes, stood behind a shallow oil-filled basin.[10] Oil of the olive found further application as an ingredient in cosmetics as well as in salves to combat afflictions that included itching blisters, chills, and numbness. It was also a base for perfumes, to be applied to the skin, hair, and clothing; used to scent rooms and outdoor spaces; and poured or burned as an offering to the gods and to the dead. On the culinary front, olive oil served as a topping for bread, as a marinade or dressing, and as a medium for cooking all manner of foods. Even the pulp that remained after pressing was valued as a pesticide and treatment for ailing trees.

In addition to such practical applications, the olive carried deep sacral resonances that extended to a wide range of social rituals, all rooted in myth. Those bearing a sprig of olive, such as supplicants and heralds, were marked as special, favored and protected by Zeus. The same was true of those who had heroically served the state as well as athletes victorious at the Olympic Games. Just how the olive came to be sacred to Zeus is explained by the Greek poet Pindar.[11] When Heracles (known to the Romans as Hercules) found the gardens of Zeus's sanctuary at Olympia bare of trees—and wished to commemorate the games he had instituted there in his divine father's honor—he brought the olive from the land of the Hyperboreans, a mythical people who, according to Pindar, inhabited regions by the Danube.

The olive was, however, sacred not only to Zeus (Roman Jupiter or Jove) but also to his daughter Athena, identified as Minerva by the Romans. Athena was patron goddess of Athens, a distinction she won in a contest with Poseidon (Roman Neptune), lord of the sea. Ovid embeds the particulars of this contest in his tale of the gifted but fatally arrogant weaver Arachne, who foolishly challenges Minerva. Here the olive, placed strategically both at the center and at the edges of the tapestry Minerva weaves, sends the unequivocal message that universal peace, justice, and order are entirely owing to the dispensation of moral gods. Minerva's message, however, is soon discredited by Arachne, whose tapestry depicts a host of mortals victimized

by wantonly lustful gods. In keeping with her tapestry's theme, the girl opts for a border of brightly colored flowers and twining ivy—emblems of Bacchus, the most changeable of gods, and signifiers of the world's unpredictability.

Attica, the region surrounding Athens, was particularly well suited to olive production, for the olive thrives especially in coastal areas with hot, dry summers. The olive became an official icon of the city, appearing as such on its coinage, together with the owl, Athena's sacred bird and symbol of that goddess's wisdom (fig. 33). Olive oil, liquid gold stored in specially produced jars, or amphorae, was given as a prize to athletes victorious in the prestigious Panathenaic Games held in Athena's honor (fig. 34). So valuable was Athena's tree that it was considered a sacrilege—punishable by banishment and confiscation of property—to desecrate the sacred olive grove that was the source of this prize oil.

Figure 33. Kalpis (water jar) with owl (detail), Greek, Athens, ca. 480–470 B.C. Attributed to the Group of the Floral Nolans. Terracotta, 35.9–36.8 × 29.5 cm (14⅛–14½ × 11⅝ in.). Los Angeles, J. Paul Getty Museum, 86.AE.229. Both the owl and the olive branches that flank it were symbols of Athena.

ΝΙΚΟΔΗΜΟΣΕΠΟΙΕΣΕΝ
ΤΟΝΑΘΕΝΕΘΕΝΑΘΛΟΝ

OVID ARACHNE AND MINERVA

Met. 6.5–145

Arachne, a girl famous for her expertise in weaving, refused to concede Minerva's superiority in that art. Her father, Idmon of Colophon, a man of lowly origins, dyed absorbent wool with Phocaean murex. Yet the girl had sought to earn a name that honored her skill and would be known throughout Lydia's cities. To admire her work, even the nymphs of Tmolus abandoned their mountain haunts, and the nymphs of the river Pactolus their customary currents. It was a pleasure not only to behold the girl's completed textiles but also to witness their creation (such beauty was there in her art), whether she was gathering the rough wool into its first balls, or working over these with her fingers to soften the wool, pulling it again and again into long threads, smoothing out the tufts, or whether turning the smooth spindle with nimble thumb: you would have sworn she had been taught by Minerva! This, however, she denied, saying, "Let the goddess compete with me!"...

Jove's divine daughter did not refuse the challenge, and without delay the two women set up their looms.... Minerva's tapestry depicted the Hill of Mars in Athens and the contest, in times of old, over that land's name. Bearing witness thereto, twice six gods sat in august majesty on lofty thrones, Jove himself in the midst. Their features, precisely rendered, identified each of them, Jove's likeness especially befitting of royalty. Minerva showed Neptune striking the Acropolis's jagged rock with his long trident, the sea spurting from the cleft, a token with which to win the city. Herself, Neptune's worthy rival, she portrayed with a shield, a sharp-tipped spear, a helmet for her head, a breastplate to protect her chest. And she illustrated how the earth, struck by her spear, produced the gray olive with its fruit (fig. 35). At the tree's miraculous appearance the assembled gods marveled. The result: Minerva's victory. And so that Arachne, as rival for her honors, might learn the price she could hope to pay for such mad presumption, the goddess added four further contests in the tapestry's four corners, bright in color and rendered with tiny figures. One corner held Thracian Rhodope and Haemus—both now being icy mountains, but once human in form—who had assumed the names of the almighty gods. Another corner had the pygmy woman's awful fate; after defeating her in a contest,

Figure 34. Panathenaic amphora (storage jar), Greek, Athens, 363–362 B.C. Attributed to the Painter of the Wedding Procession (vase painter), signed by Nikodemos (potter). Terracotta, H. 89.5 cm (35¼ in.). Los Angeles, J. Paul Getty Museum, 93.AE.55. The standard decoration on Panathenaic amphorae shows Athena, the goddess of war, armed and striding forth between columns on one side, with the inscription "from the games at Athens." The other side shows the event for which the vase was a prize.

Juno changed her into a crane and ordered her to declare war on her own people. She further depicted Antigone, who once upon a time had dared to compete with the wife of Jove; her did Queen Juno transform into a bird, a stork who applauded herself with beating wings and clattering beak. Neither Troy's royal house nor her father, King Laomedon, could prevent that. As for the remaining corner, it contained Cinyras, now childless, shown embracing a temple's steps, once the limbs of his own daughters, and weeping as he lay upon the stone. The whole, on its outer edges—the final touch—she framed with olive, the plant symbolizing peace, thus completing the work with her own tree.

Arachne, on her loom, portrayed Europa, duped by the counterfeit bull, Jupiter in disguise: you would have thought you were looking at a real bull, and real seawater, too. She could be seen gazing back at the

Figure 35. Noël Hallé (French, 1711–1781), *Dispute between Minerva and Neptune over the Naming of the City Athens.* Oil on canvas, 35 × 46 cm (13¾ × 18⅛ in.). Gray, Musée Baron-Martin

shores from which she had departed, crying out to her companions, and fearful of contact with the seething waters, timidly pulling up her feet. She also depicted Asterie, held fast by a struggling eagle, and she wove Leda lying beneath the swan's wings—eagle and swan, both were the gods' great king transformed. She added Jupiter, depicted yet again, now concealed by a satyr's disguise, impregnating Antiope with twins; then taking the form of Amphitryon when he seduced you, Theban queen; seducing you as gold, Danaë; you, Asopus's daughter, as fire; Mnemosyne, as a shepherd; Proserpina, as a serpent. She also included you, Neptune, assuming the form of a savage bull in the episode of Aeolus's daughter, later taking the form of the river Enipeus to father twin giants and the form of a ram to deceive Bisaltes's daughter. Golden-haired Ceres, most gentle bringer of crops, experienced you as a horse; Medusa with her serpents' locks, the flying horse's mother, as a bird; Melantho as a dolphin. For all these Arachne reproduced their actual appearances, reproduced in detail the settings of the crimes. Phoebus Apollo was there, in the form of a rustic farmer. He'd once worn the feathers of a hawk, another time the skin of a lion, and once had fooled Issa as a shepherd. She showed how Bacchus had tricked Erigone with bogus grapes and how Saturn, as a horse, had fathered the hybrid creature Chiron. And for her final touch, Arachne framed these scenes with a delicate border of flowers interwoven with twining ivy.

Minerva could find no fault with the girl's work. So angered was the fair-haired goddess at this outcome that she tore at that cloth embellished with celestial crimes. Holding her weaver's staff of wood from Mount Cytorus, she struck Arachne's forehead, three times, then four. Arachne, poor wretch, could not bear the blows and slipped a noose around her neck. Yet Minerva lifted her in pity as she hung suspended, saying, "You may live, you wicked girl, but keep hanging still. And lest you believe there be no further consequences, let the same terms of punishment apply also to your descendants—to the very last of them." Thereupon she departed, sprinkling the girl with a liquid drawn from Hecate's herbs. As soon as the baleful potion touched, off fell Arachne's hair, nostrils and ears as well. Her head shrank, very small, as did her whole body. Delicate limbs hung at her sides in place of arms and legs, all the rest of her a stomach from which she still spun a thread, and now having become a spider, she practiced weaving as she had done before.

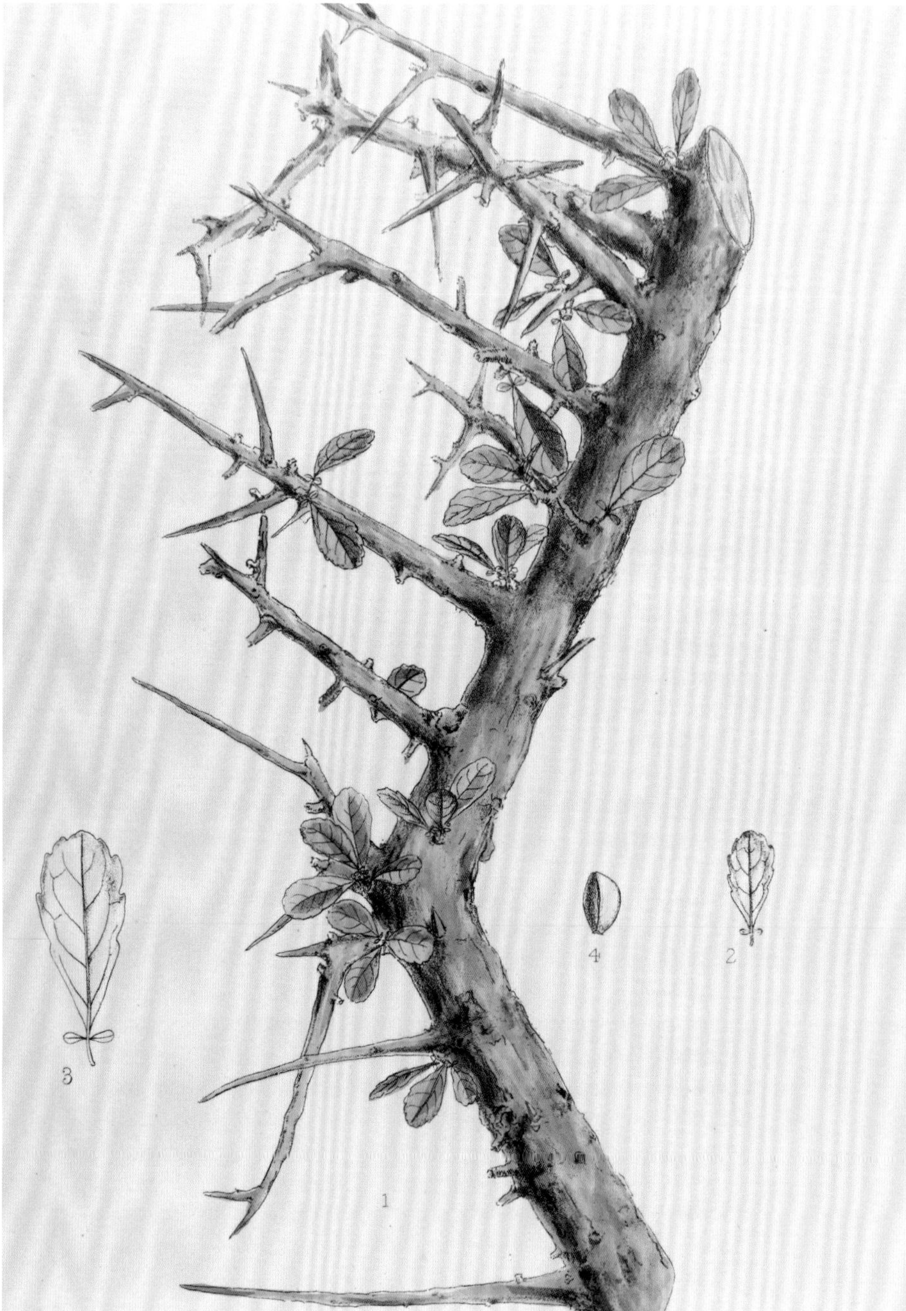

1
2
3
4

Common Myrrh COMMIPHORA MYRRHA

The common myrrh, or gum myrrh (fig. 36), one of some 250 known species of *Commiphora*, is the primary source of the incense and spice known as myrrh. Native to southern Arabia (modern Oman and Yemen) as well as to East Africa, common myrrh takes the form of a shrub or small tree up to five meters (16 ft.) in height. It is distinguished by a thick stem that allows the plant to store water efficiently. The Greek philosopher and scientist Theophrastus, drawing on the firsthand accounts of those who had accompanied Alexander the Great in his quest to conquer the Persian Empire, reports that the myrrh tree has a tough stem, thicker than a man's leg, that is twisted close to the ground. Its leaf, he writes, is spiny and not smooth.[12] It is also the case that the tree's trunk has a flaky, peeling, paperlike bark and produces knotted, spiny branches. The tree's leaves, variable in size and shape, are deciduous in autumn. Belying its humble appearance, the myrrh tree produces a sweet-smelling gum resin that seeps from fissures in its bark, occurring naturally or ensuing from damage. Such damage may result from animals chewing on it or from deliberate incisions, which, according to Theophrastus, should preferably be made at the rising of the Dog Star Sirius in midsummer and on the hottest days. When exposed to the air, this resin congeals, making it relatively easy to harvest.

It is chiefly Arabian myrrh that classical authors describe. Indeed, the Greek historian Herodotus declares Arabia to be the only country that produces frankincense and myrrh; the whole land, in fact, Diodorus adds, is scented by these trees and "exhales a wonderfully sweet odor."[13] So abundant were Arabia's aromatics that, as Strabo and Plutarch state, Alexander the Great's men used myrrh, quite extravagantly, to scent their tents and bedding as well as applying it to their skin, when exercising or in the bath, in place of olive oil.[14] This exotic region, filled with

Figure 36. David Blair (Scottish, 1852–1925), *Commiphora myrrha.* From Robert Bentley and Henry Trimen, *Medicinal Plants. . . .* (London, 1880), vol. 1, no. 60

untold riches, was aptly named by the Greeks and Romans "Fortunate Arabia" (Greek *Eudaimon Arabia*, Latin *Arabia Felix*).

Together with frankincense, myrrh was the most valuable and important commodity of those regions that produced it. Highly sought after, especially in Egypt, Persia, Assyria, Babylonia, Greece, and Rome, myrrh was conveyed north and east in ever-increasing quantities by caravans traveling overland and by sea. The trade in aromatics reached a high point in the second century A.D. with the Roman conquest of Arabia, which greatly facilitated their dissemination throughout the Roman-controlled world. And the use of aromatics was not only widespread geographically; it pervaded public and private life. For example, when myrrh was burned as incense, the sweet-smelling smoke, rising upward to the heavens, served to establish a link between people and the gods, whose favor was sought for all manner of endeavors. Myrrh was burned to honor guests invited to one's home and to scent funeral pyres of the dead, whose bodies might also be anointed with it; infamously, the emperor Nero burned more incense at his wife Poppaea's funeral than Arabia could produce in ten years' time. Myrrh and other fragrant resins were also burned to disguise the stench of blood and death at the amphitheater.

Myrrh-scented unguents were used to perfume one's hair, clothes, furnishings, and even the fur of one's pets, providing that one had the means to do so; indeed, myrrh was more important as an ingredient in the making of perfumes than as incense, since it had a stable scent, tending to fix scents that were more ephemeral. Among the host of perfumes that featured myrrh as a major ingredient were *metopium*, a scent based on bitter almonds, cardamom, rush, honey, and balsam; *regale unguentum*, containing cinnamon, cardamom, lavender, rosewood, saffron, honey, lotus, marjoram, laurel, and henna; and the delicately scented *susinum*, which was made up of lily, balsam, honey, saffron, and cinnamon. Another popular perfume, known as "Egyptian," was based on myrrh and cinnamon. Still another, called *megalion*, which contained cinnamon, frankincense, and myrrh, was valued both for its scent and its efficacy in healing wounds and reducing inflammation—for myrrh was thought to possess a wide range of health benefits. As a medicinal substance, myrrh was used to treat such relatively minor conditions as hemorrhoids and such severe ones as tetanus and kidney failure. It was employed to check excessive menstruation as well as to extract a dead fetus from the womb, and it was held to be effective in combating irritations of the mouth, trachea, and stomach. Cosmetically, too, myrrh found a great many uses. It was utilized to clear the complexion, to combat dry skin, to darken hair and stimulate its growth, and much more. Named for its bitter taste—*murr* is the word for "bitter" in Arabic—myrrh even found a place in the kitchen: it was added to wine to enhance its flavor, and wine, in turn, was said to heighten its scent.

Like all aromatics, myrrh had a special connection to Aphrodite, goddess of sensuality and love, and it is Aphrodite who, as Apollodorus tells the tale, was responsible for the myrrh tree's creation.[15] Smyrna, the beautiful daughter of Assyria's king Theias, had refused all her many suitors, thus dishonoring Aphrodite and her role in paving the road to marriage with desire. Those who dishonored the gods always paid a price, and so did Smyrna. In order to exact her vengeance, Aphrodite caused Smyrna to fall in love with her own father. Ovid, too, tells the tale of Smyrna, but casts her as Myrrha, a princess of Cyprus, and shifts responsibility for her incestuous passion from the goddess to the girl herself. The result is a story that is more tragic still, as the girl struggles between incestuous desire and the gravity of social taboo. (See also the discussion of the poppy anemone in chapter I.)

OVID MYRRHA AND CINYRAS

Met. 10.311–514

Nay, Myrrha, it was not by Cupid's shafts that the flames of your crime of love were ignited—he himself denies it! Rather with a firebrand dripping with Stygian waters and with writhing serpents in her hands did one of the Fates, those three sisters, inflame you. To hate one's father is a crime, but a sin greater than hatred was this love of yours. From all quarters noble princes desired you. For your hand, truly, the youths of all the Orient contended. Of these you should at least have chosen one, honoring that one among so many!

Myrrha, in truth, did sense the baseness of her love and fought against it: "What madness is it that moves me? What is this I plan? Oh gods and piety and a parent's sacred rights—I pray you—prevent this crime and oppose my wickedness, if wickedness it is. For piety, it is said, does not condemn such love: other animals couple without transgression. . . . What nature allows spiteful human laws prevent. Yet are there not peoples among whom mothers unite with their own sons, and daughters with their fathers? Such devotion burgeons through a twofold bond. Woe is me, not to be born there, to be injured by an accident of place! But why on such things do I dwell? Depart, you hopes for forbidden things! That man is worthy of love, a love appropriate to a father. . . ."

Thus it was she spoke. Now her noble father, Cinyras, confounded in the face of so many suitors, read out their names and asked the girl herself whose bride she would like to be. Silent at first, she burned as she looked fixedly at her father, and her eyes brimmed with warm tears. Believing this to be but a maiden's fears, he bade her to cease weeping, and dried her cheeks and kissed her lips. In this did Myrrha take delight—too much!—and when asked to decree her preference, responded, "I want a husband just like you." Not fully grasping her meaning, Cinyras responded, "May you always show such devotion!" At the mention of "devotion," the girl lowered her eyes, conscious of her guilt.

It was the middle of the night, when sleep dissolves one's cares and puts to rest the body. But Cinyras's young daughter lay awake, racked by unquenchable ardor. Her mad desires reviving, she fell into despair, feeling shame and then again desire, she knew not what to do. . . . Finding for her love neither means nor rest . . . , she resolved to hang from a noose by her own neck. Tying her belt to the doorpost's top, she cried, "Farewell, dear Cinyras. Understand the reason for my death." Then she wrapped the cord around her blanched throat.

They say that the sound of Myrrha's words reached the ears of her faithful nurse. . . . The old woman rose and threw open the doors. . . . Striking her own breast and tearing at her robe, she snatched the rope from Myrrha's neck. Weeping, she embraced the maiden, begging the reason for the noose. Mute, the girl kept silent . . . , aggrieved that her attempt at death had been thwarted. The old woman cradled her, imploring her to share her despair. . . . The girl emitted but a moan.

Determined, the nurse said, "Speak—let me be of help. . . . If you have incurred the anger of the gods, that anger can be placated by sacrifice. What else could it be? Certainly the fortunes of this house are steadfast. Your mother and your father live."

Myrrha, hearing "father," sighed from deep within her breast. Even now the nurse perceived no iniquity, suspecting only that it was a matter of the heart, and resolutely pleaded that the girl reveal whatever it was to her. Clasping the weeping girl to her aged breast and embracing her with feeble arms, she said, "I know that you are in love. In this case, too, let my care allay your fear, nor will your father ever become aware of this." At this the frenzied girl leapt from her embrace, and pressing her face to the bed, cried, "Go away, I beg of you; spare me what dignity I have left. Go or cease to ask why I sorrow. . . ." In a voice full of shame, she added, "Oh mother, how fortunate you are in your husband!" . . . At last the nurse saw the truth . . . and said, "Live. You will have your—." Not daring to say "father," she fell silent and with a nod sealed her promise.

Now all the kingdom's matrons were celebrating divine Ceres's yearly festival . . . and the king's bed was empty. Finding the king heavy with wine, the nurse—misguided by duty as she was—spoke of a certain girl's true passion for him (giving a false name), praising the maid's beauty. Asked her age, she replied, "Equal to Myrrha's." Then the king ordered the girl brought. Upon returning home, the nurse said, "Rejoice, my child, for we have prevailed!" Yet the wretched girl could feel little joy, as a foreboding lament filled her heart. Still well might she rejoice; so divided was her mind.

[Thus she came to accomplish the deed,] at the hour in which all things are silent. . . . The golden moon soon fled the sky and black clouds wreathed hiding stars, depriving the sky of its customary fires. . . . Thrice did she step back, unnerved by those signs; thrice did the grim owl ominously sing its fatal song. Yet go she did, darkness and black night having diminished her shame, feeling her way through the dark. When she reached the threshold of the bedroom, . . . the aged nurse led her by the hand to the lofty bed, and handing her over, said, "Take her, she is yours, Cinyras." Thus did she join their accursed bodies. . . .

The following night saw the deed repeated, nor was that the last. At length Cinyras, eager to know the identity of his lover after so many dalliances, brought in a light. Stunned at the sight of his own daughter and his own wicked deed, his words clotted by grief and rage, the king tore his gleaming sword from its scabbard whence it hung. Myrrha fled, prevented from being killed by favor of the night's darkness. She wandered through wide fields, leaving behind palm-bearing Arabia and Panchaia's lands. Through nine cycles of the moon did she wander when at length she rested, weary, in the Sabaean land, her womb now scarcely able to carry its burden. Caught between fear of death and weariness of life, she begged: "Oh gods, if there be any who will lend ear to my confession, though I have not deserved this lamentable punishment, I do not refuse it. But lest, surviving, I do violence to the living or, dying, pollute the spirits of the dead, exile me from both realms. So change my form thus negating both my life and death!"

There is always some deity accessible to those who confess. For as she spoke, the earth rose over her lower legs; roots bursting from her toenails spread sideways, stabilizing a tall trunk; her bones put forth wood; her blood became sap running through new wood's heart; her arms became thick branches, her fingers thinner ones; her skin hardened into bark. And as the tree grew, it enclosed her heavy womb, covered her chest, and was preparing to hide her neck. Unable to bear the delay, she sank down to meet the wood and buried her face within the bark. Though she had lost her former senses along with her body, she weeps still, warm tears trickling from the tree. In these tears resides honor: the myrrh dripping from the wood will keep its mistress's name, to be forgotten by no future age.

As her child conceived in sin had grown beneath the bark and sought a means by which to thrust itself out, the tree's middle swelled. The swollen tree, wet with falling tears, uttered moan after moan, till Lucina, gentle goddess of childbirth, came to aid those suffering branches. Splitting open, the tree produced from out its bark a child, a boy, who gave a newborn's piercing cry (fig. 37). Placing him on the soft grass, the naiad nymphs bathed him with his mother's precious tears.

Figure 37. Hans Bol, *Landscape with the Story of Venus and Adonis* (detail of fig. 22). The scene shows the birth of Adonis.

III

Piety and Devotion

2
3
4
5
6
7
8

Oak QUERCUS ILEX, QUERCUS MACROLEPIS, QUERCUS ROBUR, AND *Linden* TILIA CORDATA, TILIA EUROPAEA, TILIA SPP.

The majestic oak (fig. 38), praised in antiquity for its resilience, strength, and impressive height, was deeply revered by the Greeks and Romans alike. Long-lived—reaching several hundred years of age or even over a thousand—the oak may attain a height of forty meters (ca. 130 ft.) depending on species and growing conditions. With branches reaching the heavens, this tree logically was viewed as being sacred to Zeus, the mighty king of all the gods who lived atop Mount Olympus and the god of the sky, controlling all atmospheric phenomena.

The oak was regarded not only as sacred to Zeus but also as his incarnation, suffused with his power. This was particularly true of the famous oak of Dodona at Epirus, in northwestern Greece; the tree was one of the most famous oracles in antiquity, and reputedly the oldest oracle in Greece. Dodona attracted pilgrims for several thousand years. Those who came to ask Zeus's advice put their questions to this tree, which responded through signs—the rustling of its leaves or the calls and flight of the doves living in its branches—requiring interpretation by priests. The Greek geographer and historian Strabo reports that the sacred oak tree was revered in Dodona because it was thought to be the earliest plant created and the first to supply humanity with food.[1] This food took the form of acorns, which remained an important source of sustenance for livestock and also for poor country dwellers. Being a source of nourishment established the oak's association with the goddess of the harvest, Demeter, as well as with the earth goddess Cybele and Pan, patron god and protector of the countryside.

Figure 38. David Blair (Scottish, 1852–1925), *Quercus robur, Linn.* From Robert Bentley and Henry Trimen, *Medicinal Plants.* . . . (London, 1880), vol. 1, no. 248

These, however, are far from the oak's only ties with myth and religion (fig. 39). Zeus's wife Hera and his son Dionysus claimed this tree as being among those plants sacred to them. Oaks were sacred as well to the nymphs called dryads and hamadryads, who inhabited these trees, mingling their being with them to such a degree that the nymphs' existence depended on the trees' survival. According to a tradition preserved by Homer, Plato, and others, even humanity had close ties to the oak, which was said to have been the origin of the earliest people.[2] In the realm of heroic myth, Heracles, the most illustrious of Zeus's numerous half-mortal sons, tried to burn himself to death under an oak. Fortunately for him, Heracles was saved, freed of his sufferings, and rewarded for his many good deeds with immortality. And the goddess Athena fitted a speaking timber from the Dodona oak to the prow of the hero Jason's ship, the *Argo*, to guide and advise him. Jason's intended journey promised to be an exceedingly perilous one, for he was traveling to the eastern shores of the Black Sea in order to fetch the Golden Fleece that would secure him the throne of Iolcus, in Thessaly. The fleece hung from an oak in a grove sacred to Ares and

Figure 39. Lamp, Roman, 1st–4th century A.D. Terracotta, DIAM. 8.5 cm (3⅜ in.). Los Angeles, J. Paul Getty Museum, 83.AQ.377.150. The oak wreath serving as a decorative motif may be a reference to Jupiter, Cybele, Ceres, or the other deities to whom the tree was sacred.

was guarded by an eternally wakeful dragon. Jason ultimately secured the fleece with the aid of the princess Medea, who, using her skill in witchcraft and narcotic potions, put the dragon to sleep.

In a specifically Roman context, it was an oak upon whose branches Romulus, the mythological founder of Rome, hung the armor of his slain foe, the commander of the enemy forces of Canina. According to the historian Livy, this act proved to be of historical importance on two counts.[3] It became the first display of the so-called *spolia opima* (rich spoils), or armor stripped by one general from another on the field of battle—an exceedingly rare trophy. Indeed, over the course of their entire history, the Romans recognized only two other instances of *spolia opima* having been secured: by Aulus Cornelius Cossus, a semilegendary figure, from Lar Tolumnius, king of Veii; and by Marcus Claudius Marcellus from Viridomarus, king of the Gaesatae, a group of Gaulish warriors. The armor-decorated oak stood on the Capitoline Hill, which was subsequently chosen by Romulus as the location for a temple to Jupiter and which became the most sacred of Rome's seven hills. As Livy and other sources report, oak leaves were used to make the *corona civica* (civic crown), awarded to soldiers who had saved a comrade's life in battle. Beginning with Rome's first emperor, Augustus (r. 27 B.C.–A.D. 14), who claimed to have saved the lives of Rome's citizens by putting an end to years of civil war, wearing the civic crown became an imperial prerogative.

Apart from its divine and mythological symbolism, the oak was highly valued in antiquity as a source of shade as well as for its strong wood, widely employed in building and carpentry. Oak was used in the construction of ships, wagons, and bridges, as well as in the fabrication of columns, tools, furniture, and statuary, all objects benefiting from the use of durable wood. When burned, oak wood produced a good-quality charcoal and yielded ashes with which to flavor wine.

The linden, or lime (fig. 40), is another large, long-lived tree whose foliage provides a deep shade welcome in hot, dry Mediterranean climates. Useful as well as beautiful, the linden's wood is praised in classical sources as particularly easy to work. In his didactic poem the *Georgics*, the Roman poet Vergil describes linden wood as being both light and soft.[4] As such, it was well suited for intaglio work and turning on a lathe, and was considered necessary in the carving of statuary. Linden wood found further use in the fabrication of items such as yokes, which needed to be light and strong; spears, which should be light and smooth; architectural ornament, boxes, and chests, which required intricate carving; and portable writing tablets. The tree's pliant bark, as Horace reveals, made for an ideal base onto which a garland's flowers could be sewn.[5] Above all, the linden's value was secured by its small, fragrant, nectar-rich flowers, which were important in the keeping of bees and for honey production. The linden flower's fragrance also had a sensuous appeal that suggested this tree's affinity with Aphrodite, the goddess of love and desire.

In the realm of myth, the Greek author Apollonius of Rhodes records an obscure tale that may reflect the silver lime's spread south from Thrace and Macedonia to the Greek territory of Thessaly.[6] According to this tale, the goddess Philyra fled to Greece in shame when she was detected lying in love with the god Cronus, who would father Zeus and the other Olympian gods. In her new home, a pregnant Philyra subsequently gave birth to Chiron, the noble centaur who would become both nurse and tutor of Achilles. (See also the tale of Arachne and Minerva in chapter II.) The mythographer Hyginus adds that, horrified at giving birth to a strange species, Philyra asked Zeus to change her own form, and the god transformed her into a linden tree.[7] It is from her that the linden derived its name, for *philyra* is the Greek name for the linden.

In the *Metamorphoses*, Ovid tells an unrelated and very different tale that overtly showcases the moral integrity of a simple peasant household. And it is a tale involving both the oak and the linden. Jupiter and Mercury were traveling disguised as mortals through Phrygia, in central Asia Minor. Mercury, the Roman equivalent of Hermes, was the patron god of travelers and the agent who delivered messages between gods as well as between gods and humans. Jupiter, like his Greek incarnation Zeus, was not only the supreme god who controlled the weather but also the protector of civic order and the god who defended the sacred bond between guest and host. Particularly in Greece, the guest-host relationship lay at the heart of civilized behavior: a visitor to one's home was to be treated with dig-

Figure 40. *Tilia europaea.* From William Curtis, *Flora Londinensis: Containing a History of the Plants Indigenous to Great Britain. . . .* (London, 1828), vol. 5, pl. 615

nity, washed and fed, and presented with a gift, however humble, that would serve to establish an eternal, hereditary bond between guest and host. In the course of their travels, the two gods were everywhere refused hospitality, except by Baucis and Philemon, an elderly and impoverished couple who provided their guests all that they had to offer. For this they were rewarded, their lives miraculously and eternally transformed.

OVID BAUCIS AND PHILEMON

Met. 8.621–724 *In the Phrygian hills there is an oak next to a linden tree, both surrounded by a low wall. . . . Not far from here is a marsh, once habitable land, now shallow water filled with gulls and waterfowl. Here Jupiter once came in mortal form together with Mercury, his caduceus-bearing son, wings laid aside. Seeking a place to rest, they approached a thousand houses—firmly closed by a thousand bolts. Yet one received them. It was humble, roofed with straw and swampland reeds, but it was a house of piety. Baucis, an old woman, and Philemon, her equal in age, had been married in that same house in their younger years, and in that house grew old together, making light of their poverty, bearing it with equanimity. No distinction was there as to masters or servants; the whole household consisted of two, the same two both receiving orders and giving them.*

So when the heaven-dwelling deities reached the tiny house, and stooping, entered through the humble door, the old man brought a seat and bade them rest their limbs. Upon it attentive Baucis had spread a roughly woven blanket. Parting the warm ash in the hearth to revive yesterday's flames—feeding them with leaves and dry bark—she fanned the flames with her feeble breath. Then removing split wood and dry twigs from the rafters, she snapped them into pieces and placed them under a small brazen kettle. And she stripped the leaves of the cabbage that her husband had gathered from the well-watered garden; with a two-pronged fork she lifted the smoked hindquarters of a ham, long preserved, hanging from a darkened beam, and cutting a small part from its back, steeped the piece in boiling water. The two, meanwhile, filled the intervening time with conversation so that their guests felt no delay. A beech-wood bucket hanging from a hook by its solid handle was filled with warm water for the guests to wash their limbs. In the middle of the room a bolster of soft grasses had been placed on a couch with frame and feet of willow. This was spread with coverlets that the old couple had not used except on festal days, a humble but not inappropriate old covering. As the gods reclined, the old woman, trembling and with skirt tucked up, set up the table. Its third leg was too short, but a potshard placed underneath soon made the sloping table level. With leaves of mint she wiped it clean. The table then was set with olive, chaste Minerva's two-toned fruit, and cherries preserved in the lees of autumn's wine; endive and radish and a block of cheese, as well as eggs gently turned in hot ash, all in earthenware pots, were added. Then a mixing bowl, embossed like silverware, and cups of beech, hollowed and coated with yellow honey. The hearth soon yielded a warm meal; and wine, aged for no long time, was served again, then removed to make a little space for the final course: there were nuts, figs mixed with dried dates, plums, and fragrant apples in open baskets, and also grapes picked from purple clusters. A yellow honeycomb stood in the center. Added to all this were their kindly countenances expressing, in spite of poverty, an earnest desire to please.

Figure 41. Jean Matheus (Mathieu) (French, ca. 1592–1672), *Philemon and Baucis*. From *Les métamorphoses d'Ovide*, trans. Nicolas Renouard (Paris, 1637). Paris, Bibliothèque des arts décoratifs

Alas, each time the mixing bowl was drained, they saw it refilled, the wine's level rising of its own. Awestruck at this strange occurrence, their hands uplifted, Baucis and Philemon prayed fearfully, begging pardon for their simple meal and lack of preparation. Now there was a single gander, guardian of that tiny house, whom the couple were preparing to slaughter for the visiting deities. Swift of wing, he led them on, long eluding their grasp—slow as they were from age—till at length he appeared to take sanctuary with the gods. They forbade that he be killed. "We are gods," they said, "and while this wicked neighborhood will receive its just deserts, you will be granted immunity from all harm. Just leave your house and follow our steps, accompanying us onto the mountain's steep slopes." They both obeyed, and with the support of staffs, set one foot before the other on the long rise. At the distance from the summit of a discharged arrow's flight, they looked back and saw everything covered with water; their house alone remained. And while they marveled at all this, lamenting their own fate, that old house, small even for its two owners, was transformed before them into a temple. Columns replaced the poles supporting its gable, its roof of thatch began to glisten, and the earthen floor was changed for marble, doors embossed and roof made gold.

Then did Jupiter speak full placidly: "Tell us noble old man, and woman worthy of so noble a husband, what you wish for." After speaking briefly with Baucis, Philemon conveyed their joint desire to the gods: "We ask to be priests and guardians of your temple; and since we have lived our lives together, let a single hour take us both so that I may never gaze upon my wife's tomb nor be buried without her." Forthwith their prayers were honored: they became the temple's guardians for their remaining years. Having completed the full course of their lives, while they chanced to stand before the temple's steps and recall what had happened to this place, Baucis watched Philemon sprout a covering of leaves, and Philemon, older by a bit, watched Baucis sprout leaves as well (fig. 41). As the treetops grew above their faces—while it was still possible—they spoke to each other, and just as soon as they uttered "Farewell, my spouse," their mouths were sealed by verdant growth. To this day, a Bithynian can point out two tree trunks there side by side, formed from their two bodies.

IV

Mortals in Love

1
2
3
4
5
6
7
8
9
10
11
12
13
14
15
16
17
18
19

Black Mulberry MORUS NIGRA

Native to southwestern Asia, the black mulberry (fig. 42) is a rounded, deciduous tree that may reach a height of twelve meters (39 ft.). Known in Greece at least by the fifth century B.C., the mulberry has heart-shaped leaves with rough upper surfaces and soft undersides. The Roman naturalist Pliny the Elder writes that the mulberry was called "sapientissima arborum" (wisest of trees), since it produces its foliage in the late spring when the danger of damaging frosts has abated.[1]

Classical authors make limited reference to mulberry wood, which appears to have been used in construction and the carving of statuary. The Greek philosopher and botanist Theophrastus also mentions the employ of mulberry wood to make the hoop or framework for wreaths of flowers.[2] While we know few specifics about ancient uses of mulberry wood, a great deal of information has been preserved about this tree's raspberry-like fruit, which found an extensive range of applications. Turning from green to red and then to dark purple, the mulberry is best consumed when fully ripe and was notoriously difficult to keep fresh, since the berries' juice readily ferments. It is in order to prevent the berries' souring that ripe mulberries are optimally gathered from the tree before the sun becomes "oppressive," as the Roman poet Horace recounts.[3]

Juice from the mulberry was used to flavor and color red wine, and if taken with wine (notes Pliny the Elder) was found to neutralize the noxious effects of aconite and spider venom as well as to relax the bowels and to expel intestinal parasites. Applied to the cheeks, mulberry juice was used cosmetically as rouge. Mulberry leaves could be applied directly to alleviate burns, and when boiled with bark of black fig and grapevine, yielded a dye for hair. Macerated in urine,

Figure 42. David Blair (Scottish, 1852–1925), *Morus nigra, Linn*. From Robert Bentley and Henry Trimen, *Medicinal Plants*. . . . (London, 1880), vol. 4, no. 229

mulberry leaves were used to remove the hair from hides. As for the mulberry's root, juice extracted from it was found to alleviate toothaches, and a mouthwash was produced by boiling the root with squill vinegar and earthworms.[4]

The Greek epic poet Pherenikos connects the mulberry with a nymph named Morea who inhabited this tree—thus the plant's Greek name, *morea*.[5] Beyond this bit of lore, however, and Ovid's moving story of Pyramus and Thisbe, two star-crossed young lovers from Babylon, not a great deal of mythology survives that pertains to the mulberry.

OVID PYRAMUS AND THISBE

Met. 4.55–166

Pyramus and Thisbe, he the handsomest of youths and she the finest of all girls in the Orient, had neighboring houses where Semiramis is said to have built a city fortified with a wall of baked brick. Proximity promoted their acquaintance and first affections: their love grew over time. They would have joined in marriage by the nuptial torch, but their fathers prevented it. One thing they could not prevent: both lovers burned alike with enraptured minds. When no one was there to see, they conversed through nods and signals, and the more their love's flame was hidden, the brighter that hidden fire burned.

The wall shared by the two houses was split by a narrow crack formed when the wall was built. Throughout the long years, no one had noticed that flaw. But what does love not discern? You lovers were the first to see it and made of it a passage for your words. Through it your talk of love, uttered in lowest whisper, could travel safely. Often, when they had taken up their positions by the wall—Thisbe on one side and Pyramus on the other—and each in turn had listened for the other's breath, they would remonstrate, "Cruel wall, why do you stand in the way of lovers? How small a thing it would be for you to allow us to meet face to face. If this is too much, might you allow us to exchange kisses? But we are not ungrateful. We know we are beholden to you for our words' passage to the ears of our beloved." Such things were said in vain, so sitting each in separate spots, they said "Farewell" at nightfall and to the wall gave kisses that never reached the other side.

After dawn had displaced the stars of night and the sun's rays had dried the dewy grass, they met at the usual place. Then after much hushed complaint, the pair decided to elude their guardians in the quiet of night and try to meet outside their doors, leaving behind their homes and city; but that they might not get lost in the spreading countryside, they would meet at the tomb of Ninus, taking shelter in the shadow of a tree. At that place grew a tree heavily laden with white fruit, a tall mulberry next to a cool spring. This plan, they agreed, was a good one. And when finally the sun plunged into the sea—departing with a painful slowness—night rose at long last from those same waters. Opening the door, with face concealed, clever Thisbe made her exit through the darkness, escaping detection by her household, and arriving at the tomb, took a seat beneath the special tree. Love made her bold. All of a sudden—look!—a lioness, her foaming jaws blood smeared from a recent slaughter of cattle, came to slake her thirst in the waters of the fount. By the light of the moon, Babylonian Thisbe saw her from afar and fled in fright to a gloomy cave, leaving behind a veil that had slipped from her shoulders. The fearsome lioness, meanwhile, having with a deep drink of water satisfied her thirst, made her way back into the forest. By chance she came upon the veil, lying there without its owner, and tore at the delicate cloth with those bloodied jaws.

Pyramus, having set out later, came upon a wild beast's unmistakable footprints in the deep soil. A pallor then overspread his entire face. When next he found the blood-stained garment, he lamented, "A single night will claim the life of two lovers, though of the two she was most deserving of a long life; mine is the guilty heart. It is I, poor girl, who have been your ruin, I who bade you go by night to places full of fear. Would I had arrived earlier! Rend my body and devour my guilty inner parts with your ferocious jaws, you lions that live beneath this crag. But merely to hope for death is a coward's way!" Lifting Thisbe's veil, he took it with him to the shadow of their tree. Covering the precious garment with tears and kisses, he exclaimed, "Now receive a deep draft of my blood!" The sword, that weapon hanging at his side, he plunged into his body. Then drawing the blade from the gushing wound, he lay flat on his back upon the ground. Blood spurted up high, as when a pipe of brittle iron ruptures and emits tall shafts of water hissing through the narrow opening, breaking through the air with violent surges. The tree's fruit, spattered with blood, darkened, and the blood-soaked roots further stained the hanging mulberries a purple hue.

But now, though her fear had not yet abated, Thisbe returned, unwilling to fail her beloved, straining with eyes and mind to detect him, eager to tell him of the dangers she had narrowly avoided. Soon she spotted the place and shape of the tree. But the fruit's strange color made her uncertain. As she wavered, she saw quivering limbs strike the ground. Drawing back, her face paler than boxwood, she trembled like a water's surface ruffled by a gentle breeze. In a moment, she recognized her beloved and struck her innocent chest and tore her hair in loud lamentation. Holding his body in her arms, she filled his wounds with weeping, mixing blood with tears and covering his face in kisses. "Pyramus," she cried, "what mishap has taken you from me? Pyramus, answer me! It is your beloved Thisbe who calls you; listen and raise your fallen face!" At the mention of Thisbe's name, he lifted his eyes heavy with death, and having glimpsed her, lowered them again.

Recognizing her own veil and seeing his scabbard without its sword, she said, "It was your own hands and your love that ruined you, unlucky one! I, too, have a hand brave enough for this one task; love I, too, have. Love will give me the strength for fatal wounds. I will accompany you in death and in my utter misery will be called both cause and partner of your passing. Alas, you whom only death could separate from me, even in death will not be torn from me. Oh pitiable parents, mine and his, both our voices join in this one request of you: begrudge not to lay to rest in a single tomb those whom unshakable love and premature end have joined. But you, oh tree that shades the poor corpse of one and is soon to shade the other's, keep the marks of shed blood and forever bear dark fruit, so suitable for mourning, as a memorial of a twofold death." Thus she spoke, and placing the iron sword's tip still warm from the blood just shed beneath her breast, fell upon it (fig. 43; see also fig. /). Her prayers reached the gods and reached her parents as well: for the fruit is still dark in color when ripened, and what remained of them from the funerary pyre rests in a single urn.

Figure 43. Lucas Cranach the Elder (German, 1472–1553), *Pyramus and Thisbe*, 1515–20. Oil on panel, 58 × 39.2 cm (22⅞ × 15 7/16 in.). Bamberg, Neue Residenz

Apple MALUS DOMESTICA

Cultivated apple varieties (fig. 44), hybrid in origin, were a typical orchard fruit in the classical world. The domestication of apples may have begun in Anatolia, the Asian portion of modern Turkey, but the plant's precise history is still unknown and much debated. In Roman imperial times, some thirty varieties of apple were known. Evolved in part by grafting, many, according to Pliny the Elder, were introduced by individuals who had governed overseas provinces.[6]

Eaten fresh or dried, apples could be made into a strong cider or wine. The Greek physician Hippocrates, however, cautions against eating fresh apples, as they are hard to digest, though he does recommend the juice of apple as a remedy for intestinal disorders.[7] Recognizing that sweet and sour apples affect digestion differently, Galen, physician to the emperor Marcus Aurelius, promotes fresh, sweet apples, citing their importance to a healthy diet; other varieties are to be baked.[8] For the Romans, apples served as a suitable finish to a banquet, and the gourmet Apicius records recipes for apples preserved in honey as well as for a pork-and-apple *minutal*, or ragout.[9]

In mythology the apple had a long symbolic and religious association with fertility and sexual passion—though it should be noted that both Greeks and Romans sometimes used the word "apple" to describe a range of fleshy fruits, including the quince and pomegranate, which introduces an element of uncertainty to identifications, particularly in mythological references. Given their connection with fruitfulness and desire, in Greece apples served as gifts at weddings and engagements, and appear as love tokens in both Greek and Latin literature. For instance, the mythographer Hyginus writes that the earth goddess Gaia originally produced the apple tree as a wedding gift for Zeus and Hera, the latter deity representing women as wives

Figure 44. Joris Hoefnagel (Flemish/Hungarian, 1542–1600), *French Rose and Apple*, 1591–96. From Georg Bocskay, *Mira Calligraphiae Monumenta* (Vienna, 1561–62), Ms. 20, fol. 107. Watercolors, gold and silver paint, and ink on parchment, 16.6 × 12.4 cm (6 9/16 × 4 7/8 in.). Los Angeles, J. Paul Getty Museum, 86.MV.527.107

and mothers.[10] Hera would later persecute Heracles, one of Zeus's numerous illegitimate offspring, and set in motion his completion of the famous Twelve Labors. One of these involved gathering golden apples from Gaia's original tree, growing in a sacred grove in the far west, at the ends of the earth. This tree was tended by the Hesperides, daughters of the Evening Star Hesperus, and was guarded by a serpent (fig. 45; see also fig. 9). Cunningly, Heracles let the Hesperides's neighbor Atlas fetch the apples in his stead—something Atlas was happy to do, as Heracles offered to relieve him temporarily of his own eternal task of carrying the full weight of the heavens on his shoulders.

The most infamous apple of all is the golden apple inscribed with the words "for the fairest" that the goddess of strife, Eris, brought to the wedding of Peleus and Thetis, the future parents of Achilles. Angered that of all the gods she alone had been omitted from the guest list—and seeking her revenge—Eris knew that more than one goddess would covet this prize. Indeed, Athena, Hera, and Aphrodite all claimed it, with tragic results. The three goddesses approached the Trojan prince Paris, the handsomest of mortal men, to judge their respective merits, each offering him a bribe. The most enticing bribe was that offered by Aphrodite: Helen, wife of the Spartan king Menelaos, the most beautiful woman in the world. Helen's subsequent abduction by Paris, and the Greeks' fervent desire to retrieve her, led to the Trojan War.

A third widespread myth, likewise involving golden apples, is that of Hippomenes and Atalanta, the latter famed for her skill in hunting, her beauty, and her speed. Atalanta would agree to marry only that man who could outrun her, a thing that none could do. Those who tried and failed would be penalized with death. The goddess Venus herself narrates this tale in Ovid's dramatic version.

Figure 45. Red-figure lekythos (oil flask) with garden of the Hesperides, Greek, Athens, ca. 420–400 B.C. Attributed to the Circle of the Meidias Painter. Terracotta, H. 19.7 cm (7¾ in.). Los Angeles, J. Paul Getty Museum, 91.AE.9

OVID ATALANTA AND HIPPOMENES

Met. 10.560–680

Perhaps you may have heard of a certain girl who outshone the swiftest of men in running races; and that rumor was no fiction—for she was faster. Nor could you say whether she was more notable for the fleetness of her feet or the beauty of her person. When she consulted the oracle about a husband, it replied: "Atalanta, you have no need of a husband. Hasten from the bonds of marriage. Yet you will not escape, and though still alive, you will lose your spirit, the essence of your being." Terrified by the prophecy, she lived alone, unmarried, in the shady woods. Aggressively she drove away a throng of suitors, by stating a condition: "No one will possess me who has not first outrun me. So race with me—a wife and bed of marriage will be the swift man's prize, but for the slow, the prize is death. Let these be the rules of the contest." Cruel was she indeed, but so great was the draw of her beauty that a crowd of impetuous suitors came despite these terms.

Now Hippomenes had taken a seat merely as a spectator of this unfair race, and mocking the youths' excessive love, asked, "What kind of man seeks to win a spouse in the face of such great dangers?" But when he saw Atalanta's face and figure, once her cloak was flung aside, . . . he was thunderstruck, and raising his hands, said, "You whom I have just now criticized, I beg your pardon! I had not yet seen the prize that you sought." His praises flamed his passion's fire, and though fearing self-reproach, he hoped that no youth would outrun her. "Yet why is my luck untested in this contest?" he wondered aloud. "Do not the gods themselves favor the bold?" As Hippomenes pondered, the maiden flew by on winged feet; and though in the eyes of this Boeotian youth she appeared to fly as quickly as a Scythian arrow, he admired her beauty all the more—the running made her beautiful. Her robe blew back from her speeding feet, her hair tossed on her ivory neck, the bands of colored threads streamed out beneath her knees. Over her pale young body a flushed glow spread, no different than when a crimson awning suspended over an atrium of gleaming white casts a blushing shadow. While the stranger noted all this, the final lap was run, and victorious Atalanta was crowned with a celebratory wreath.

Yet undeterred by the others' fate, the youth stood in the arena's midst, his eyes fixed on the maiden. "Why do you seek an easy victory by defeating weaklings? Match yourself against me," he said, "to see whether fortune makes me supreme; you will not be ashamed to be defeated by such as me. For my father is Onchestius, Neptune's grandson, and I am great-grandson of the waters' king. Nor is my courage any less than expected from one of my birth; if I am defeated, your name will be celebrated and remembered for Hippomenes's defeat."

As he spoke, Atalanta, King Schoeneus's daughter, looked at him with a kindly expression, and unsure whether she would prefer to be defeated or be victorious, spoke thus: "What god, prejudiced against the handsome, wishes to destroy this youth and bids him seek this marriage without any thought for precious life? In my judgment, I am not worth so much. Nor am I moved so much by his beauty (though I could be moved by this as well) but because he is still a boy: it is not he himself but rather his age that moves me. What does it matter that he has courage and a spirit unafraid of death? What does it matter that he is the fourth descendant from a watery deity? What does it matter that he's in love and holds marriage with me so dear that he would face death should heartless fate deny me to him? While you still can, stranger, depart and abandon that bloody marriage bed. Marriage with me is cruel. There is no girl who wouldn't want to marry you; be yourself desired by a sensible girl! Oh, why then do I care so much for you, when so many have died before? Let him take heed! Let him then die, since he has been unmoved by the deaths of so many suitors and tires so of life. Will he die then, since he wanted to live with me and suffer an undeserved death as love's price? My victory will not come without a hatred that must be endured. But the fault lies not with me. If only you were willing to desist! Or since you are clearly mad, I wish that you were the faster! But how innocent the look on his boyish face! Oh poor Hippomenes, I wish you had not seen me. Deserving of life you were; had I been luckier and not denied marriage by the grim Fates, you alone were the one with whom I would have wanted to share a marriage bed." So she spoke, and being inexperienced—now first touched by desire—she knew not what she was doing: she was in love and failed to see it.

Now the crowd and her father both demanded the usual race when Hippomenes, Neptune's descendant, called out, begging: "Cytherean goddess, Venus, I pray you watch over my bold deeds and assist those flames you have ignited." A breeze bore these sweet prayers to me, inclined as I was to listen; and I was moved, I confess it, nor was help long in coming. There was a field, which the inhabitants call Tamasus, Cyprus's most fertile zone. Men of old had consecrated this to me and ordered that, as a gift, it should be added to my sanctuaries. At the field's center glows a tree with golden foliage, rustling branches of flaming gold. Coming from there, I happened to be carrying three golden apples, picked by my own hand. Seen by no one except Hippomenes himself, I approached and instructed him how these could be used. The horns blared the signal, and leaning forward from the starting gate, each runner leapt forward, like a

Figure 46. Guido Reni (Italian, 1575–1642), *Atalanta and Hippomenes*, 1618–19. Oil on canvas, 206 × 297 cm (81⅛ × 116 15/16 in.). Madrid, Museo Nacional del Prado

flash of light, grazing the sand's surface with swift foot: you would think they could have traversed the waves with unwet feet and skimmed across stalks of silver grain. Shouts bolstered the youth's spirits. "Now, now, hurry to increase your pace, Hippomenes!" coaxed the onlookers. "Now use all your strength! No more hesitation! And you will win." It is uncertain whether in these words Megareus's son or Schoeneus's daughter rejoiced more. Oh, how often, when she might have passed him, did she hang back, unwilling to leave behind those features she had long studied. Dry came the breath from his weary mouth, and the finish still a long way off. At length, Neptune's descendant cast one of the three apples. The maiden was amazed, and desirous of the shining fruit, she ran off course and plucked up the rolling gold. Hippomenes raced ahead, and applause erupted from the audience. Correcting for the delay and wasted time, Atalanta began a sprint, leaving the youth once more at her back. Then again, detained by the casting of a second apple, she fell behind, again by the youth was caught and passed (fig. 46). Now, with only the final stretch of the course remaining, he cried, "Come to my aid, goddess, granting me the prize!" He threw the shining gold sideways with all his youthful strength to the far edge of the field, whence her return would be protracted. Seek the apple or not? She seemed not to know. I, goddess of love, compelled her to pick it up, adding to the apple's weight when lifted. Due equally to the obstacle's weight and the delay—lest my story run longer than the race—the maiden was passed: the victor led off his prize.

V

A Guided Walk through Ovid's Garden

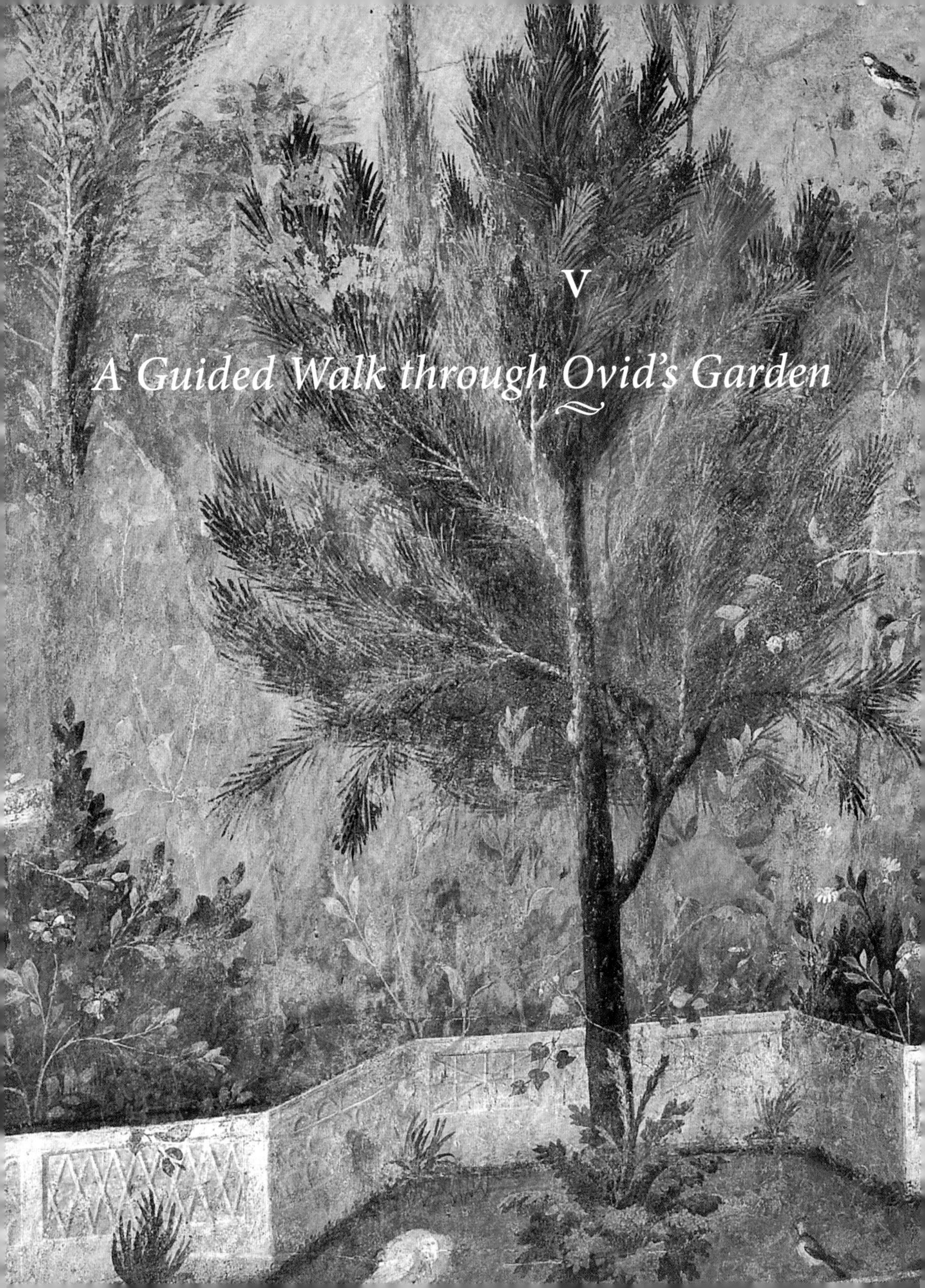

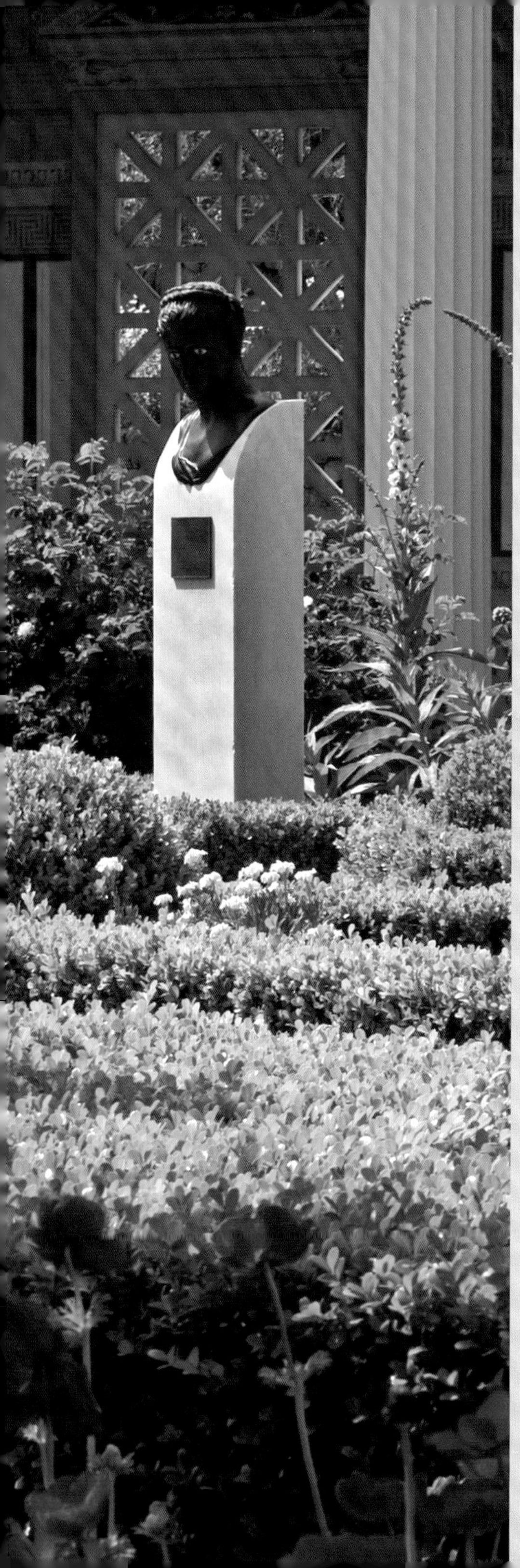

The tales recounted in the previous chapters—those of Daphne, transformed into a stately laurel; Hyacinthus, commemorated by a fragrant bloom; and fleet Atalanta, entrapped by an apple's golden glow—are among the best known of Ovid's botanical myths, but they do not represent his full poetical spectrum. Rather, the *Metamorphoses* mirrors a vast botanical garden blooming with diverse species from the far reaches of the earth. The species contained in Ovid's garden range from the mysterious mushroom, a potentially deadly delicacy, to barley, a humble but vital cultivated plant. His array includes aconite, a poisonous flower on the Black Sea's eastern shores; frankincense, a shrub found in Arabia and Africa; and crocus, which to this day yields a precious dye. These plants and others, their mythologies less well known or told in the *Metamorphoses* but briefly, are collected here. And as in an actual botanical garden, Ovid's flora bear identifying "tags" for the enjoyment of those visitors who wish to linger over them, contemplating their storied role in the gardens of ancient Greece and Rome.

Here begins the walk . . .

ACONITE • ACONITUM LYCOCTONUM, ACONITUM NAPELLUS (*Met.* 7.404–24)

The aconites that the Greeks and Romans knew likely included *Aconitum lycoctonum* and *Aconitum napellus*, both erect perennials of European origin with dark-green leaves and growing to one and a half meters (5 ft.) in height. Bearing the common names of wolf's bane and monkshood, these aconites produce distinctive hooded flowers in mid- to late summer, and all parts of the plant are highly toxic. Flowers of the *lycoctonum* species may be yellow or purple, while those of *napellus* are indigo blue. Plants called "aconite" in antiquity may also have included specimens of a different genus, specifically the species now known as *Doronicum pardalianches*, or great leopard's bane, a plant that can be found not only in Greece and Italy but also in northwestern Asia Minor. Great leopard's bane, belonging to the aster family, grows to a height of ninety centimeters (35 in.) and bears light yellow flowers from late spring to midsummer. It, too, is toxic.

Given its toxicity, aconite was a popular poison in antiquity. Its most famous victims included Aristotle, who administered it with his own hands when, at the age of seventy, he was indicted for impiety. As Pliny the Elder reports, its alleged antidotes were diverse: garlic, rue, milk with balsam oil, warm sheep's milk, castoreum (derived from the testes of a beaver) mixed with milk or water, or a broth of old rooster with a little salt.[1] In the realm of myth, Ovid recounts that the sorceress Medea used aconite in her attempt to kill young Theseus, who would become the founder-king of Athens, but her ruse was discovered just in time. Medea had brought this poison from her home on the eastern shores of the Black Sea. Aconite, the plant from which her poison was derived, sprang up from the foam falling to the ground from Cerberus's mouth when Hercules, performing one of his famous labors, dragged the struggling, triple-headed dog from its home in the underworld into the light of day.

BARLEY • HORDEUM VULGARE (*Met.* 5.448–61)

The importance of barley as a source of food for humans and animals alike is directly reflected in its ubiquitous use in sacrifice to the gods. Thus barley features prominently in one of the earliest descriptions of sacrificial ritual to appear in Western literature: in Homer's *Odyssey*, the hero can make contact with the spirits of the dead only by digging a pit into which he must pour an offering of milk mixed with honey, wine, and water, all sprinkled with white barley and saturated with fresh sheep's blood.[2]

Barley, the oldest cultivated grain in Greece, was among the main products of Mediterranean agriculture. One of the first plants domesticated by Neolithic farmers in the Fertile Crescent, it spread from the Near East to the Aegean—and thereafter to the Balkans, central Europe, the western Mediterranean, and Egypt. Tolerant of drought and able to be grown in acid, sandy soils, barley was produced in abundance throughout Greece, though it was particularly well suited to Attica, the region surrounding the city of Athens. While a staple food for most Greeks, who consumed it in the form of porridge, puffs, and rough cakes, barley as a source of human food was of relatively minor importance in Roman Italy, where it was considered more suitable as fodder for animals. The physician Galen comments that barley porridge was the customary food of armies in classical Greece, but that among Roman soldiers it was considered a punishment. That is not to say, however, that Romans uniformly disdained barley; the gourmet Apicius provides recipes for ham boiled with barley and figs as well as for several barley soups.[3]

In myth and religion, barley was most closely associated with Ceres, goddess of grain and the harvest. Appropriately, barley is integral to the most important myth involving Ceres, namely the abduction of her daughter Persephone by Pluto, god of the underworld. (See also the discussions of the pomegranate and the narcissus in chapters I and II, and the discussions of the Madonna lily and the violet below.) As Ovid tells the tale, Ceres roamed the earth in search of her daughter, and greatly wearied, stopped to rest at a cottage. Here she was offered a sweet drink containing barley kernels. When a rude boy mocked the goddess for her greediness, she threw her drink at him in a rage. The grains of barley spotted his face, and he became a reptile, smaller and more insignificant than a lizard.

CROCUS • CROCUS CARTWRIGHTIANUS, CROCUS SATIVUS (*Met.* 4.283)

A perennial growing to five centimeters (2 in.), *Crocus cartwrightianus*, native to Greece and Crete, produces fragrant goblet-shaped flowers in shades of lilac or white with purple veins. Having prominent red stigmas, these flowers appear in autumn and early winter. This crocus is the ancestor of the extensively cultivated saffron crocus, *Crocus sativus.* Autumn flowering, *Crocus sativus* bears rich lilac flowers with deep purple veins, also with conspicuous red stigmas.

The saffron crocus, with its yield of precious spice and pigment, was a plant of great religious and economic significance in the ancient Mediterranean, and had been so at least as early as the Bronze Age. It appears front and center in fresco paintings from Bronze Age Crete and Santorini dating from the second millennium B.C. Among them is a famous painting from the Palace of Minos, at Knossos, representing a blue monkey (which the palace's excavator, Sir Arthur Evans, thought to be a blue boy) picking crocus flowers. Akrotiri, an ancient site on the island of Santorini, has yielded frescoes depicting young women, perhaps priestesses, picking crocus flowers in the presence of a divinity, as well as a narrative frieze that shows a procession of boats adorned with garlands of crocus.

It is the flowers' stigmas that, picked by hand, are the source of saffron. Produced locally by the Romans but also extensively imported from the Near East—the best, as Pliny the Elder states, came from Cilicia (the southern coast of Asia Minor)—saffron was an ingredient in cooking, flavoring both wine and sauces, and in the making of perfumes for personal as well as public use; for instance, the Roman poet Lucretius recounts the use of saffron mists to spray the stage in the theater.[4] Cosmetically and medicinally, saffron also proved versatile. It was employed as an eyeliner, hair lightener, and ingredient in the coveted body lotion *helianthus*. Praising saffron for its range of medicinal applications, the elder Pliny recommends it as a treatment for afflictions of the eyes, stomach, chest, kidneys, liver, lungs, and bladder as well as for the ill effects of inebriation.[5] As a dye, saffron yellow was a mark of royalty and distinction. Saffron-colored robes were worn by the priests of the mother goddess Cybele, by the young girls participating in coming-of-age rituals in the sanctuary of the goddess Artemis at Brauron, and also by mythological heroes or heroines and gods, perhaps most famously the goddess of the dawn, Aurora, whom Homer describes as being "krokopeplos," or clad in a saffron-colored robe.[6]

The saffron crocus was linked to a host of deities, including Demeter; Hecate, goddess of witchcraft; the Erinyes, spirits of vengeance; and Hera and Zeus, beneath whom, as Homer writes, a carpet of crocus bloomed as they lay in love.[7] As for the crocus flower's origin, Ovid alludes to the story—its details obscure—of Crocus, who like his spurned admirer Smilax, was transformed into a plant subsequently bearing his name. In an alternate account of this flower's origin, Crocus was a youth loved by Mercury who, like Narcissus, was fatally wounded while competing at the discus throw and in death was memorialized by a flower. (See also the discussions of the hyacinth and the narcissus in chapters I and II, and the discussion of the smilax on pp. 130–131.)

CYPRESS • CUPRESSUS SEMPERVIRENS (*Met.* 10.106–42)

Native to the eastern Mediterranean, the cypress is a columnar or conical evergreen tree that produces small cones and is distinguished by branches bearing sprigs of tiny scaled leaves. Growing to heights of some thirty meters (ca. 100 ft.) and reportedly capable of living as long as a thousand years, the cypress was the source of an exceptionally hard wood used principally for the construction of ships, sarcophagi, and temple doors. This tree was sacred to a wide range of deities, including Apollo, Artemis, Aphrodite, Hermes, Persephone, the healing god Asclepius, whose staff was made of its wood, and Zeus, whose birthplace on Mount Ida, in Crete, was notable for its presence. Although the cypress had strong symbolic connections with birth and life, it also became closely associated with funerary practices and was planted in cemeteries. As Ovid recounts, the cypress arose from a young prince named Cyparissus, dearly loved by Apollo. The prince wished to end his life in grief over the death of his pet stag, shot accidentally by his own arrow, and was transformed by the god into the cypress tree so that, as a funerary plant, the youth might mourn eternally.

FRANKINCENSE • BOSWELLIA CARTERII, BOSWELLIA SACRA (*Met.* 4.190–255)
Deciduous and generally multistemmed, the frankincense tree is native to the Arabian Peninsula as well as to East Africa. Potentially reaching a height of eight meters (26 ft.), frankincense trees are found in desert woodlands, usually on rocky limestone slopes and in ravines. Their peeling, papery bark and gnarled branches give these trees a distinctive appearance befitting their extraordinary value, for these trees are the source of the precious oleo-gum-resin frankincense, which exudes from fissures in the bark. When burned, this resin produces a scent that the geographer Strabo characterizes as "a most perfect incense."[8] And burned it was—in ever-increasing quantities—largely in honor of the gods, whose favors were desired for all manner of undertakings. Indeed, the popularity of frankincense as an incense was rivaled only by its great desirability as an ingredient in medications, perfumes, and cosmetics.

That frankincense trees are notoriously difficult to grow in any but their native habitat ensured that they remained highly prized exotics, engendering both fabulous tales and unquenchable desire. In one fable that enjoyed much credence in antiquity, the Greek historian Herodotus recounts that Arabian frankincense trees (to his knowledge, they grew in Arabia alone) are closely guarded by small, multicolored, winged serpents that must be dispelled by heavy smoke before the fragrant resin can be harvested.[9] Among those wishing to gain both firsthand knowledge and, ultimately, control of frankincense's sources was Alexander the Great, who sent a fleet to explore the coasts of Arabia for this purpose. In Theophrastus's observations of this expedition, he also recounts that the sailors, taking advantage of the local Sabaean tribe's trusting nature, surreptitiously made off with an abundance of frankincense.[10] According to Alexander's biographer Plutarch, the conqueror sent great quantities of frankincense home to his boyhood tutor in Macedonia, one Leonidas, who had chided him for throwing incense on the altar fire with both hands, saying: "You can be so lavish with incense only when you have conquered the spice-bearing regions." This shipment of frankincense was accompanied by a message from Alexander: "And now you may cease to be so stingy with the gods!"[11]

As Ovid reveals, frankincense had particular ties to the sun god Helios. In vengeance for Helios's exposing the love affair between Venus and Ares, Venus caused Helios to fall hopelessly in love with the lovely Leucothoe, whom he pursued relentlessly, ignoring his former lover Clytie. (See also the discussion of the heliotrope below.) The scorned and angry Clytie then broadcast Helios's new affair, taking pains to inform Leucothoe's father, who subsequently buried his daughter alive. Unable to revive Leucothoe and heartbroken at her loss, Helios caused a fragrant shrub, frankincense, to rise from her body as it melted away.

HELIOTROPE, COMMON • HELIOTROPIUM EUROPAEUM (*Met.* 4.234–70)

Native to Europe, Asia, and North Africa and favoring dry, sandy, open habitats, this annual plant is widely naturalized. Low growing to a height of fifty centimeters (20 in.), the common heliotrope has gray-green branched stems rough to the touch and hairy oval gray-green leaves. Dioscorides likens its leaves to those of basil, though they are rougher, larger, and darker in color.[12] In summer the common heliotrope produces numerous spikes of sweet-scented white or pale lilac flowers that, according to Dioscorides, look much like the winding tail of a scorpion. Appropriately, he recommends a decoction of heliotrope, either drunk in wine or applied topically, for the treatment of scorpion stings. Believed to be a very useful plant from a medicinal perspective, it was worn as a necklace to serve as a contraceptive, and its seeds, smeared on the skin, were used to dry up warts, pustules, and other unpleasant growths. The heliotrope's leaves, ground and applied topically, were employed to treat the symptoms of gout and sunstroke, and they were also used to induce abortions.

Ovid vividly describes the heliotrope's origin. Clytie was a nymph loved by the sun god Helios. When Helios cast her off for another, an agonized Clytie languished, with no thought for food or drink or for taking shelter in the heat of day and the dark of night. She focused only on the sun, never averting her gaze, and took root where she sat, her body becoming but a small flower that always turns its gaze adoringly to the sun. (See also the discussion of frankincense on pp. 121–122.)

LILY, MADONNA • LILIUM CANDIDUM (*Met.* 5.392)

Native to southeastern Europe and the eastern Mediterranean, the Madonna lily produces fragrant white trumpet-shaped flowers five to eight centimeters (2–3 in.) in length, from late spring through summer. This lily has a long history in the arts of Greece, appearing as early as the Bronze Age on the island of Crete, and it is also one of the plants depicted most frequently in Roman frescoes. Although the lily grows wild, it was extensively cultivated in antiquity, as it was a flower favored for making crowns and garlands as well as for the creation of perfumes.

In religious thought, the lily had a particular association with Hera, goddess of marriage and childbirth. It may be for this reason that the lily was considered especially useful in treating the ailments of women. For instance, the Greek physician Soranus writes in his work on gynecology of the efficacy of lily oil in the treatment of hysterical suffocation, obstructed respiration resulting from a uterine condition.[13] In conjunction with the lily's ties to Hera, the flower became a symbol of virginity, a thing soon to be lost, as well as of fertility and marriage.

In the realm of myth, the lily, alluring for its beauty and its scent, was linked to several infamous cases of abduction and rape. According to the Greek poet Moschus, Europa, the daughter of the king of Tyre, was picking lilies, her favorite flower, when she was abducted to the island of Crete by Zeus, who enchanted her by changing his form into that of a lovely tame white bull.[14] And, as Ovid tells the story, the goddess Ceres's daughter Persephone was picking white lilies and violets when Hades, god of the underworld, burst from the depths of the earth to take her for his queen. (See also the discussions of the pomegranate and the narcissus in chapters I and II, and the discussions in this chapter of barley and the violet.)

LOTUS • NELUMBO NUCIFERA, NYMPHAEA CAERULEA, NYMPHAEA LOTUS, OR NYMPHAEA STELLATA (*Met.* 9.336–54)

In classical antiquity several different plants were known as "lotus." Among them are the date palm, *Diospyrus lotus*, and a deciduous shrub in the buckthorn family, the jujube, or *Zizyphus lotus*, widely believed to be the source of the fruit that the mythical Lotus Eaters offered to Odysseus's men. Although honey-sweet, the fruit posed a danger, for those among Odysseus's men who tasted it would want to stay with the Lotus Eaters, becoming forgetful of all their woes but forgetful also of the homecoming that they had coveted for nearly twenty years.[15] Both the date palm and the jujube have been put forward as Ovid's lotus, but they do not correspond to his description of the plant.

In Ovid's story, a young woman named Dryope, one of the god Apollo's several loves, approaches a lake near which the water lotus bloomed in hues of Tyrian purple. Picking some of these lovely flowers as amusement for her young son, she discovers that the flowers are bleeding, the branches or stalks from which they had been picked quivering in horror. For the lotus had but recently been Lotis, a girl pursued by the lustful nature god Priapus and saved from his advances only by a timely metamorphosis. (See also the discussion of the poplar below.)

The most likely candidates for Ovid's water lotus are the sacred or Indian lotus, *Nelumbo nucifera*, and various species of *Nymphaea*, or water lily. These plant choices have been dismissed by literary scholars on the grounds that the lotus and water lily grow *in* a lake, not "near to one," as Ovid states. However, the water lily and lotus grow rooted in the sediments of bodies of water, but do not grow in water over two and a half meters (8 ft.) deep. In other words, they grow in shallow water, often found at the marshy edges of a lake. The sacred lotus and water lily are fruit bearing, and their flowers can take on a color that could be described as a shade of Tyrian purple: the sacred lotus's flower can be pink; that of the Egyptian white water lily or white lotus, *Nymphaea lotus*, a pink-tinged white; that of the Egyptian blue water lily or sacred blue lily, *Nymphaea caerulea*, mauve; and that of the so-called red-and-blue water lily or star lotus, *Nymphaea stellata*, purple, mauve, or fuchsia. Regularly confused by classical authors who did not have firsthand knowledge of them, the lotus and lily were closely identified with Egypt, where they were regarded as sacred, becoming a familiar motif in both Egyptian carving and painting.

MINT • MENTHA AQUATICA, MENTHA ARVENSIS, MENTHA LONGIFOLIA, MENTHA SPICATA (*Met.* 10.728–29)

Water mint, field mint, horsemint, and spearmint are all species of mint known to and cultivated by both Greeks and Romans. Intensely aromatic herbaceous perennials with distinctive square-shaped stems, these mints are native to Europe and parts of Asia. Ranging in height from ten to a hundred centimeters (4–40 in.), they spread by underground rhizomes and bear purple, pink, or white flowers in whorls. Depending on species, their green leaves may be serrated at the margins and hairy.

The mint family, rich in essential oils, found an extraordinarily wide range of applications in antiquity. Decorative and fragrant garden plants, mints were used to make garlands and chaplets as well as to flavor wine and all manner of foods. The Roman gourmet Apicius lists mint as a key ingredient in sauces for fowl, boar, venison, pork, shellfish, and fish as well as in the preparation of vegetables, including side and main dishes of lentils, peas, pumpkin, cabbage, mashed vegetables—and, of course, fruit-based desserts. As Pliny the Elder asserts, the aroma of mint filling the air typified rustic feasts.[16] Mint was also employed in the treatment of a host of illnesses. In *On Medicine*, for example, the Roman encyclopedist Celsus speaks of mint's efficacy in the cure of diseases and afflictions of the liver, intestines, tongue, stomach, nostrils, and mouth as well as in relieving irritations of the skin resulting from spider bites and scorpion stings.[17]

As for the origins of mint, Ovid mentions in passing a story that is told in greater detail by the geographer Strabo and others.[18] Ovid says that Persephone, upset that her husband, Pluto, had some interest in a nymph named Minthe, trampled her to the ground, leaving her in the form of the plant that bears her name. Mint thereafter became linked with the worship of Persephone and her mother, Demeter, goddess of the harvest. (See also the myth of Venus and Adonis and that of Baucis and Philemon, as well as the discussions of the pomegranate and the narcissus, in the previous chapters, and the discussions of barley, the Madonna lily, and the violet in this chapter.)

MUSHROOM • AGARICUS CAMPESTRIS, AND OTHER SPECIES (*Met.* 7.390–93)

Being fungi, and not actually plants, mushrooms were regarded with wonder: lacking seeds and roots, they seemed to come into being spontaneously. Pliny the Elder cites "mud, soil suffused by fermenting liquid, and the wet roots of acorn-bearing trees" as the "cause and origin" of fungi, which begin their existence as a delicate foam.[19] And according to Athenaeus, who himself cites Theophrastus, the frequency and violence of thunderclaps directly influences mushrooms' size and abundance.[20]

There is evidence that mushrooms were gathered from the wild and consumed in Italy as early as the Bronze Age, and that the Romans recognized that mushrooms were not enjoyed without risk. Pliny the Elder mentions the notorious case of the emperor Claudius's untimely death as a result of eating a dish of poisonous mushrooms—all the doing of his wife Agrippina.[21] Pliny goes on to say that only country dwellers who are in the habit of gathering mushrooms really know which are poisonous and which are not: not only are certain types of mushroom inherently poisonous; all are also subject to being tainted if, for example, they grow near pollutants such as rusty iron, rotten cloth, or serpents' lairs. This being said, mushrooms were regarded as a delicacy. Pliny duly supplies guidelines for those determined to cook them: avoid eating those that become hard in cooking. Those that soften when cooked, though, should be safe, particularly if boiled with some meat or the stalks of pears. He adds, however, that it is a good idea to eat pears after a meal of mushrooms in every instance, as pears, like vinegar, neutralize mushrooms' poison. In spite of the dangers, mushrooms were also used for medicinal and cosmetic purposes. Certain mushrooms were believed to aid digestion, and others, applied topically in washes, were used to treat dog bites and ulcers as well as to diminish freckles and other blemishes.

Ovid tells a strange story about mushrooms, one unique in classical literature. After engineering the death of the Thessalian king Pelias, who held the throne belonging rightfully to her husband, Jason, the sorceress Medea fled to the city of Corinth. On her way, she passed the spring Peirene, where at the beginning of time human beings had sprung from rain-soaked mushrooms.

PINE • PINUS HALEPENSIS, PINUS NIGRA, PINUS PINEA (*Met.* 10.103–4)

The pine, a familiar coniferous evergreen, was a common sight in classical antiquity in coastal regions, on mountains, and in gardens. Of the large number of pine species found throughout the Mediterranean, the most widespread is the Aleppo pine, *Pinus halepensis* (12–20 m, or 39–65 ft.), often found in coastal regions. Another coastal pine is the distinctively shaped stone or umbrella pine, *Pinus pinea*, which is described by Vergil as favored for planting in gardens.[22] Although the wood of the stone pine was of poor quality for building, the tree was highly valued for nuts from its cones. Most useful for the construction of buildings and ships were the straighter-growing, stronger mountain pines, among them the black pine, *Pinus nigra*. Theophrastus specifies that because pine resists decay, it was the preferred wood for the building of merchant ships, which stayed in the water for long periods of time.[23] In the case of warships, by contrast, where speed and maneuverability were paramount, the preferred timber was fir, a less durable but lighter wood.

Pine was also the source of pitch, or resin, an extremely valuable commodity in antiquity. Pitch was used in shipbuilding to seal the joints of boards and to cover hulls, where it served both as waterproofing and flame retardant—particularly helpful when under attack by an enemy shooting flaming arrows. Pitch was also invaluable in the production and distribution of wine. Ceramic vessels storing wine during shipment were sealed with pitch, which inevitably flavored the wine. Far from being considered an impurity, pitch was regularly added to wine to enhance its flavor. Pitch had a range of medical and cosmetic applications as well; it could serve as a depilatory and was used as an ingredient in the making of perfumes and of medicines to treat the symptoms of diseases as diverse as gout, consumption, and ulcers.

Given pine's importance in the building and finishing of ships, it is not surprising that the tree was considered sacred to Poseidon, god of the sea. And as a vigorous evergreen used in the production of wine, it was sacred to Dionysus as well. The pine was associated, too, with the nature goddess Cybele, who became infatuated with a handsome youth named Attis. Discovering Attis's intention to marry, Cybele attacked the tree in which his beloved, a tree nymph, resided. Fatally wounded, the nymph passed away, and a grief-stricken Attis became so distraught that, in a fit of madness, he castrated himself. Ovid relates this much of the tale in his work the *Fasti*, but adds in his *Metamorphoses* that Attis subsequently became a pine.[24] (See also the discussion of the violet below.)

POPLAR • POPULUS ALBA, POPULUS NIGRA (*Met.* 2.340–66; 9.324–93)

Favoring moist woodlands and the banks of streams and rivers, both black and white poplars are fast-growing deciduous trees that can reach a height of thirty-five to forty meters (ca. 115–130 ft.). Native to Europe, southwestern and central Asia, and northwestern Africa, the black poplar, *Populus nigra*, is distinguished by its dark bark and triangular to ovate glossy dark-green leaves. The white poplar, *Populus alba*, is native to Africa, Turkey, and the central and southern portions of the former USSR, including parts of Siberia. Its dark-green leaves have a fuzzy white underside, and its trunk and bark are a striking white as well.

The Roman architect Vitruvius lists poplar as a wood useful for building, a statement substantiated by Cato in his recommendations for maximizing the productivity of farmland.[25] Cato advocates the planting of poplar on the border of one's farm and alongside roads, as this tree is a good source of timber and at the same time an excellent source of fodder for sheep.

As the black poplar produces only small seeds and unobtrusive flowers, it was viewed as infertile and accordingly linked with death and the underworld. Thus when in the course of his wanderings it is time for Odysseus to consult the deceased prophet Teiresias, who alone can tell him how to reach his home, the hero must travel to the Grove of Persephone, which abounds in willow and poplar: here he will find access to Hades's house.[26] And Pliny the Elder reports that the followers of the philosopher Pythagoras, who believed in the transmigration of the soul, were buried covered in leaves of the black poplar.[27] Although the white poplar was sacred to the sun god Helios and accordingly linked with light and life, it, too, had funerary associations. As Pausanias writes, the hero Heracles brought the white poplar from the underworld, where he had gone to fetch the triple-headed dog Cerberus, guardian of the dread House of Hades.[28] (See also the discussion of the aconite earlier in this chapter.) When the hero later made sacrifice to his father, Zeus, at the sanctuary of Olympia, he burned the poplar's wood, and from that time on, it was this wood alone that was burned at Olympia in Zeus's honor. The white poplar became sacred to Zeus and to Heracles, and was sacred also to Dionysus. These deities, and their celebrants, might all wear wreaths of poplar.

There are several accounts of the poplar's origin. According to Servius, Hades created the first white poplar as a memorial to Leuke, a lovely nymph whom he had brought to the underworld, upon her passing.[29] Ovid writes that the black poplar originated with the princess Dryope, who became this tree as a punishment for picking the crimson flower of the lotus, itself a nymph transformed. (See the discussion of the lotus earlier in this chapter.) Not specifying white or black, Ovid also writes that in the extremity of their grief, the sisters of Phaethon became poplars, their bodies enclosed entirely in bark and ever shedding tears—the amber worn by Roman brides. It was Phaethon who had driven the sun god's chariot so erratically as to threaten heaven and earth alike, prompting Jupiter to end his life.

REED, GIANT • ARUNDO DONAX (*Met.* 1.676–712)

Giant reed is a robust perennial grass that, growing to a height of five meters (16 ft.), is the largest grass in Europe. Once thought to be indigenous to the Mediterranean basin, giant reed is now believed to be Asiatic in origin, despite long cultivation and naturalization in the Mediterranean. Like bamboo, giant reed grows in many-stemmed clumps, spreading aggressively from underground rhizomes. Also like bamboo, its individual culms, or stems, are strong and hollow; however, the reed's long, narrow, tapering leaves clasp the culm at their base, and the reed produces plumes of whitish flowers from summer to early fall.

The uses of giant reed in antiquity were many. It could be planted as a windbreak or boundary fence, and its culms harvested as fishing rods, walking sticks, braces for grapevines, supports for vaulting and roofs, writing instruments, arrows, straws through which to administer medication, and handy devices for removing out-of-reach cobwebs from inside the house. Giant reed was also employed to construct bridges for the harplike instrument known as the lyre and to make the flute known to the Greeks as the syrinx. In the story that Ovid relates, Syrinx was a lovely nymph who fled the nature god Pan's advances. Asking to be rescued from his relentless pursuit, Syrinx was transformed into a clump of reeds. Still desiring her, Pan gathered these reeds and bound them together with wax to form the first reed pipe.

SMILAX • SMILAX ASPERA (*Met.* 4.283)

Smilax, also known as rough bindweed, is a creeping or climbing evergreen with some resemblance to ivy. Pliny the Elder points out in his *Natural History* that the common people regularly mistook smilax for ivy and employed it to make wreaths to wear in the worship of Dionysus.[30] Scholars, however, doubt that the use of smilax resulted simply from error, as a range of vigorously growing vines was sacred to this god. The smilax, which can be found growing in Mediterranean Europe, Asia, central Africa, and Mexico, was reputedly introduced to Greece from Cilicia, Asia Minor's southern coastal region.

Distinguished from ivy, the stems of the smilax bear spines, and its leathery dark-green leaves—heart-shaped, with toothed and spiny margins—also bear spines on the midrib of their underside. From August to September the smilax produces white, highly fragrant flowers, described by Pliny as scented like lilies. Pliny also remarks that the smilax's berries, red deepening to black and borne in clusters, are comparable in appearance to grapes.

In the *Metamorphoses*, Ovid mentions the origin of the smilax only in passing. From Pliny the Elder we know the story is an unhappy one: Smilax's love for the youth Crocus being unrequited, this maiden was transformed into the plant that bears her name. (See the discussion of the crocus earlier in this chapter.)

VIOLET • VIOLA FRAGRANS, VIOLA GRACILIS, VIOLA ODORATA, VIOLA SPP. (*Met.* 5.392)

Of the five hundred or so known species of violet, a number were undoubtedly known to and actively cultivated by the Greeks and Romans, who had a great fondness for this flower. In classical literature the violet is described as fragrant, delicate, and black—in reference to its deep purple color—but also as white or yellow. Dioscorides likens the leaf of the violet to that of ivy, though thinner and darker in color.[31] Its flower, he writes, is small, sweet smelling, and purple. In fact, violets do come in a range of colors. The *Viola fragrans*, a relatively rare Greek wildflower, usually blooms yellow, though it can also be white or pale violet. The *Viola gracilis*, which is native to the Balkans, Greece, and Turkey, produces deep violet flowers, and only occasionally yellow ones. Native to most of Europe, the so-called common, English, sweet, or garden violet, *Viola odorata*, generally produces deep purple flowers, though white, pink, pale blue, and yellow forms are also known.

The violet, planted in domestic gardens for the captivating scent it produces, was a flower favored in the making of chaplets and garlands, for which purpose it was actively cultivated in market gardens. There were, however, numerous other reasons for treasuring the violet. Pliny the Elder recommends that, along with roses, lilies, poppies, and thyme, violets should be planted for one's bees with the aim of producing particularly flavorful honey. And in the realm of medicine, Dioscorides writes of the purple violet's cooling faculty; its leaves, when applied with polenta, can ease a burning stomach and inflammations of the eyes. The elder Pliny adds that, by virtue of their fragrance, chaplets of violet cure headaches caused by drunkenness, among other things. Imbibed with water, the purple violet cures epilepsy in children, and its seeds ease the sting of a scorpion. Yellow and white violets, he writes, are no less useful, being suitable to treat gout, abscesses, and a host of other ailments.[32]

In myth and religion, the violet had ties with a range of deities. Both Aphrodite and Dionysus are described in literary sources as being crowned with garlands of violets; in the words of the poet Pindar, the Muses were believed to have dark, lustrous hair the color of this flower; and in Homer's *Odyssey*, violets grow profusely in a meadow on the paradisiacal island of the seductive nature goddess Calypso.[33] As Ovid writes, violets also grew on the meadow where Persephone was gathering flowers when Hades abducted her. Accounts of the violet's origin include the Christian apologist Arnobius's assertion that this flower sprang from the severed member of the goddess Cybele's beloved Attis, who, crazed by grief, had castrated himself. More violets, Arnobius adds, grew from the blood of Ia, who, upon hearing the news of her betrothed Attis's demise, took her own life.[34] (See also the discussions of the pomegranate and the narcissus in the previous chapters, and the discussions of barley, the Madonna lily, and the pine in this chapter.)

NOTES

Introduction

1. *Theogony* 187–98.
2. *Letters to Atticus* 4 and 5.
3. Nonnos, *Dionysiaca* 41.118–25.
4. *Metamorphoses* 7.404–24.
5. *Tristia* 2.207.
6. *Tristia* 1.7.22, 1.762, 1.763.

I. Gods in Love

1. *Guide to Greece* 10.5.
2. *Historical Miscellany* 3.1.
3. *Odyssey* 7.115.
4. *Satyricon* 31.
5. Natural History 21.84, 23.58, 23.60, 30.16; 23.16, 13.2; 20.82, 22.70, 23.42, 23.43, 23.57, 29.11; and 24.54, 23.58, respectively.
6. *Gynecology* 1.62.
7. See, for example, the so-called Homeric *Hymn to Pan* 26; *Odyssey* 6.231; *De materia medica* 4.63.
8. *Iliad* 14.348.
9. *Natural History* 21.94.
10. *De materia medica* 2.207.
11. *Natural History* 21.94.

II. Hubris and Human Excess

1. *De medicamina faciei* 63.
2. *De materia medica* 4.161; *Natural History* 21.75.
3. *Apicius* 7.12.3.
4. Homeric *Hymn to Demeter* 7.
5. *The Bacchae* 273–85.
6. *Natural History* 14.
7. Book 5 "On Wines," passim.
8. *Guide to Greece* 9.12.3.
9. *Letters to His Brother Quintus* 3.1.5.
10. *Guide to Greece* 5.11.10.
11. *Olympian Ode* 3.
12. *Enquiry into Plants* 9.4.3, 9.1.6.
13. *The Persian Wars* 3.107; *Library of History* 3.46.1.
14. *Geography* 15.2; *Life of Alexander* 40.
15. *The Library* 3.14.4.

III. Piety and Devotion

1. *Geography* 7.2.
2. *Odyssey* 19.163; *Republic* 8.544.
3. *From the Founding of the City* 1.10, 10.46.
4. *Georgics* 1.160.
5. *Odes* 1.38.2.
6. *Argonautica* 2.1230–41.
7. *Myths* 138.

IV. Mortals in Love

1. *Natural History* 16.53.
2. *Enquiry into Plants* 5.6.1–3.
3. *Satires* 2.4.21–23.
4. *Natural History* 23.70, 23.71, 30.8.
5. *Deipnosophists* 3.78b.
6. *Natural History* 15.5.
7. *On Regimen* 2.55.
8. *On the Properties of Foodstuffs* 6.594–98.
9. *Apicius* 1.20, 4.3.4.
10. *Astronomica* 2.3.

V. A Guided Walk through Ovid's Garden

1. *Natural History* 20.23, 20.51, 23.47, 29.33, 32.13.
2. *Odyssey* 11.23–36.
3. *On the Properties of Foodstuffs* 1.11.2; Apicius 7.9.3, 4.4.1, 4.4.2, 5.5.1, 5.5.2.
4. *Natural History* 21.17; *De rerum natura* 4.54.
5. *Natural History* 21.81.
6. *Iliad* 8.1.
7. *Iliad* 14.348.
8. *Geography* 14.4.19.
9. *The Persian Wars* 3.107.
10. *Enquiry into Plants* 9.4.5.
11. *Life of Alexander* 25.
12. *De materia medica* 4.193.
13. *Gynecology* 3.28.
14. *Moschus (Europa)* 2.32.
15. *Odyssey* 9.82–102.
16. *Natural History* 19.47.
17. *De medicina* 4.4, 4.10, 4.12, 4.15, 4.18, 4.24; 5.27, 6.8.
18. *Geography* 8.3.
19. *Natural History* 22.46.
20. *Deipnosophists* 2.60.
21. *Natural History* 22.46, 22.47.
22. *Eclogues* 7.65, 7.68.
23. *Enquiry into Plants* 5.7.1.
24. *Fasti* 4.222–46.
25. *On Architecture* 2.9.5; *On Agriculture* 6.3.
26. *Odyssey* 10.509–10.
27. *Natural History* 35.46.
28. *Description of Greece* 5.14.2.
29. *Vergilii carmina commentarii*, commentary on *Eclogue* 7.61.
30. *Natural History* 16.63.
31. *De materia medica* 4.122.
32. *Natural History* 21.41; *De materia medica* 4.122; *Natural History* 21.76.
33. *Pythian Odes* 1.1; *Odyssey* 5.72.
34. *Adversus nationes* 5.7.

Atlantic Ocean
Gaul
Spain
Italy
Adriatic Sea
Rome
Vesuvius
Herculaneum
Pompeii
Bay of Naples
Tyrrhenian Sea
Sicily
Syracuse
Mediterranean Sea
Africa
Tomi
Black Sea
Thrace
Macedonia
Greece
Athens
Aegean Sea
Lydia
Asia Minor (Anatolia)
Phrygia
Rhodes
Crete
Cyprus
Syria
Phoenicia
Alexandria
Egypt
Nile
Red Sea
Arabia
Caspian Sea
Assyria
Mesopotamia
Babylon
Persia
Pasargadae
Persian Gulf
0 250 mi
0 400 km

Macedonia
Thasos
Mt. Olympus
Troy
Dodona
Thessaly
Aegean Sea
Lesbos
Chios
Delphi
Boeotia
Thebes
Attica
Athens
Corinth
Peloponnese
Olympia
Sparta
Delos
Naxos
Cnidus
Rhodes
Thera (Santorini)
Cythera
0 50 mi
0 50 km
Mt. Ida
Knossos
Crete

GLOSSARY

Acheron. River in the underworld and the name of the god of this river. He is the father of Ascalaphus, Proserpina's betrayer.

Aelian (Claudius Aelianus; ca. A.D. 170–235). Roman rhetorician and author of *Historical Miscellany*, a cultural-historical work in Greek that is filled with moralizing anecdotes and short biographies of illustrious personages as well as descriptions of the world's natural wonders and diverse cultures.

Aeolus. Keeper of the winds and father of a girl named Canace.

Ajax. Greek hero who fought in the Trojan War. He took his own life in shame when Achilles's armor was awarded to Odysseus (Ulysses) instead of to him. Ovid refers to an alternate tradition regarding the hyacinth's origin according to which a purple flower sprang from the hero's blood.

Amphitryon. Husband of Alcmene, who would become the mother of Hercules.

Antigone. The Antigone depicted in Minerva's tapestry was a member of Troy's royal family, not the daughter of Theban king Oedipus.

Antiope. Daughter of a Theban king who was imprisoned and cruelly treated for bearing "illegitimate" offspring.

Aphrodite. Greek goddess of love and desire, closely associated with gardens and fertility in general. Plants sacred to her included the rose, myrtle, and poppy anemone. The Romans identified her with the goddess Venus. See also *Cytherea*.

Apicius (1st century B.C.–4th century A.D.?). The name by which several proverbial Roman gourmets are known. This name is used primarily in reference to a collection of recipes, *On the Art of Cooking*, which appears to have been assembled over the ages by a number of authors and is impossible to date accurately.

Apollo. God of prophecy, light, healing, music, and archery. The plant most sacred to him was the bay laurel. Apollo became identified with the sun god Helios, and as god of light, he was given the name Phoebus.

Apollodorus (1st or 2nd century A.D.). The name that, likely in error, has become associated with the authorship of *The Library*, an encyclopedic summary in Greek of Greco-Roman myth and legend.

Apollonius of Rhodes (1st half of the 3rd century B.C.). Author of the Greek epic poem *Argonautica* (Voyage of the *Argo*), centered on the hero Jason's quest for the Golden Fleece.

Ares. Greek god of war, identified by the Romans with the god Mars.

Arethusa. Spring near Syracuse in Sicily. It is called "Pisaean" because the water nymph Arethusa, after whom the spring is named, had lived in Pisa, a district of the city of Elis in Greece, but fled from there to Sicily when pursued by the river god Alpheus.

Arnobius (act. ca. A.D. 295–330). Rhetorician in the Roman province of Numidia, in North Africa, during the reign of the emperor Diocletian. Upon converting to Christianity, he authored a work entitled *Adversus nationes* (Against the pagans).

Artemis. Greek goddess of the hunt and protector of animals, associated with childbirth among both animals and humans. Her haunts were forests, meadows, and other wild places. She was known to the Romans as Diana.

Asopus. River god who was father to Aegina. Her son by Jupiter, Aeacus, would name an island after her.

Asterie. Daughter of two Titans, a generation of gods preceding that of Jupiter.

Athena. Patron goddess of the city of Athens. She was the Greek goddess of wisdom and of defensive war as well as patron goddess of craftspeople such as weavers, potters, carpenters, and sculptors. The plant most sacred to her was the olive. The Romans knew her as Minerva.

Athenaeus (act. ca. A.D. 200). Author of a fictional account in Greek of one or more dinner parties in Rome. The work, whose title is variously translated as *The Connoisseurs in Dining* or *Learned Diners*, recounts the guests' conversations about food and a variety of other subjects.

Aurora. Goddess of the dawn.

Avernus. Lake at the entrance to the underworld. In the story of Pluto and Persephone, Ovid uses the name simply as a reference to the underworld, where the water nymph Orphne lived.

Bacchidae. A ruling caste of the city of Corinth who founded the Sicilian city of Syracuse.

Bacchus. Roman equivalent of the Greek god Dionysus.

Bisaltes. Son of the sun god Helios and Gaia (the earth). His daughter was Theophanes.

Bithynia. Kingdom and Roman province in the northwest of Asia Minor located just north of Phrygia on the Black Sea.

Boeotia. Region of Greece north of Athens and the Gulf of Corinth.

Capitoline. The most sacred of Rome's famed seven hills; victorious generals celebrating a triumph made sacrifices here.

Cato, Marcus Porcius (234–149 B.C.). Roman statesman and military figure who rose to prominence in Rome's wars against Hannibal and Carthage. He was a staunch advocate of traditional lifestyles, morality, and government. His writings include *On Agriculture*, which covers topics including the cultivation of olives, grapes, and other fruit as well as pasturage for domesticated animals.

Cayster. River of Lydia (modern Turkey) noted for its swans.

Celsus, Aulus Cornelius (act. ca. A.D. 14–37). Author of an extensive encyclopedia in Latin covering subjects that included agriculture, philosophy, warfare, and rhetoric. Only the eight books on medicine survive.

Cephisus. God of a river of this name in central Greece and father of Narcissus.

Ceres. Roman equivalent of the Greek goddess Demeter.

Chiron. A centaur born of the nymph Philyra.

Cicero, Marcus Tullius (106–43 B.C.). Preeminent Roman statesman, orator, philosopher, and political theorist of the late Republic. His copious writings include works on rhetoric, philosophy, theology, and political theory as well as personal letters, poems, and political speeches. He was executed on the orders of Mark Antony and Octavian (Augustus).

Cinyras. Legendary king of Cyprus. His daughters were transformed into the steps of a temple, presumably because they had challenged that temple's presiding deity.

Claros. City on the Ionian coast sacred to Apollo and site of a famous oracle.

Cnidus. Coastal city of Caria, in Asia Minor, and a center of Venus's worship.

Colophon. Coastal city in Asia Minor that fell under Lydian control.

Columella, Lucius Junius Moderatus (ca. A.D. 4–70). Practicing farmer and author of a systematic treatise in Latin on agriculture including soil management, production of field crops, and viticulture.

Cronus. Child of Gaia and Uranus (the sky). Cronus overthrew his father to become king of the gods and was in turn overthrown by his own son Zeus. Other deities that he fathered include Hera, Poseidon, Demeter, and Hades. Both the Greeks and the Romans knew him by the name of Cronus, but the latter also identified him with Saturn.

Cupid. Roman equivalent of Eros.

Cyane. Spring near Syracuse, in Sicily.

Cybele. Asiatic nature goddess known as the Great Mother whose popular cult was introduced to both Greece and Rome.

Cythera. Island off the southern coast of Sparta, ostensibly the location of Venus's emergence from the sea and therefore island of her birth. It was the site of a temple to Aphrodite (Venus) Ourania, or "Heavenly Aphrodite."

Cytherea. Name for Venus referencing her connection to the island of Cythera.

Cytorus, Mount. Mountain in Anatolia that was the standard source of boxwood, considered one of the best woods for turning.

Danaë. Daughter of Acrisius, king of Argos. Although imprisoned in a tower by her father, she was impregnated by Jupiter, who gained access to her in the form of a shower of golden rain. She became the mother of the hero Perseus, famous for beheading Medusa.

Delos. Island of Apollo's birth.

Demeter. Greek goddess of grain, the harvest, and the fertility of the earth in general. Identified by the Romans with Ceres.

Diana. Roman patron goddess of wild things who became identified with the Greek goddess Artemis.

Diodorus (act. ca. 60–20 B.C.). Known as Diodorus Siculus, "the Sicilian." He authored an extensive history of the known world from mythical times to Caesar's conquest of Gaul. His work, written in Greek, includes discussions of Egypt, Mesopotamia, India, Scythia, Arabia, North Africa, Greece, and Europe.

Dionysus. Greek god of vegetation as well as of wine and the release it provides. The Romans identified him with Bacchus.

Dioscorides, Pedanius (ca. A.D. 40–90). Author of a major pharmacological work in Greek reflecting an extensive knowledge of medical botany and prognostics.

Dis. Another name for Pluto.

dryad. Tree nymph.

Enipeus. River in Thessaly and corresponding river god. Disguised as the latter, Neptune sired two giants known as Otos and Ephialtes.

Enna. City in central Sicily.

Erebus. Another name for the underworld.

Erigone. Athenian girl who, with her father, had welcomed Bacchus and the new culture of wine; the amorous episode to which Ovid appears to refer, in the story of Arachne and Minerva, is not otherwise known.

Eros. The child-god of love. Armed with bow and arrow with which to incite love, he was the son of Aphrodite. The Romans identified him with Cupid.

Etna. In Ovid's story of Pluto and Persephone, a reference to the notoriously active Sicilian volcano Etna.

Etruscans. People of northwestern Italy, whose precise origins are disputed. The Etruscans and their territories were absorbed by Rome and her growing empire.

Euripides (485?–406 B.C.). Together with Aeschylus and Sophocles, one of the most famous Greek tragedians. Among his best-known plays are *The Bacchae* and *Medea*.

Europa. Daughter of the king of Tyre. Jupiter approached her in the form of a tame white bull, and once she had climbed onto his back, took her away to Crete.

Eurotas. Main river in the territory of Sparta.

Fates. Three divine sisters who determined a person's destiny.

Gaia. Greek goddess who personified the earth.

Galen (A.D. 129–?216). One of the most eminent physicians in the Roman world. He rose from gladiators' physician to court physician under the emperor Marcus Aurelius. Having served both the emperors Commodus and Septimius Severus, he died during the reign of Caracalla.

Hades. Greek god of the underworld. He was called Dis by the Romans but was also known to both the Greeks and the Romans as Pluto, "the wealthy one," since all things come to him after death.

Hecate. Goddess associated with the lower world, ghosts, magic, potions, poisonous plants, and the night, particularly the witching hour.

Hera. Greek goddess of marriage and childbirth. Wife of Zeus and queen of the gods, Hera was patron goddess of women, watching over them particularly as wives and mothers. The Romans identified her with the goddess Juno.

Heracles. Son of the god Zeus and the mortal woman Alcmene, this hero, blessed by prodigious fortitude and strength, became famous for completing twelve daunting labors.

Hercules. Roman name for Heracles.

Hermes. Greek god responsible for delivering messages between gods and mortals as well as for conducting the souls of the dead to the underworld. Befitting his role as messenger, Hermes wore winged sandals and a broad-rimmed traveler's hat. In his hands he carried the caduceus, a magical staff entwined with two serpents that served as an emblem of his office as herald and guide of the dead. Identified by the Romans with Mercury.

Herodotus (ca. 480–425 B.C.). Known as the "father of history," he was the first to make the events of the past the subject of investigation. His history in Greek of the Greco-Persian Wars (490–479 B.C.) contains a wealth of geographical, mythological, political, and ethnographic information.

Hesiod (act. ca. 725 B.C.?). According to Greek tradition, the author of two highly influential, instructional epic poems: the *Theogony*, which treats the origins of the universe and of the gods, and the *Works and Days*, which includes reflections on social and religious conduct as well as a farmer's calendar.

Hesperus. The evening star.

Hill of Mars. Called the Areopagus in Greek. It lies northwest of the Acropolis and was once the meeting place of the city's highest court for cases of murder or religious infractions.

Hippocrates (ca. 460–370 B.C.). Renowned Greek physician considered to be the founder of Western medicine. While a number of letters and speeches are plausibly attributed to him, the so-called Hippocratic Corpus—works on subjects including physiology, internal medicine, gynecology, surgery, and dietetics—

is likely a compilation from numerous authors.

Homer (8th century B.C.?). According to Greek tradition, author of the *Iliad* and the *Odyssey*, together the earliest extant examples of literature in the Western world.

Horace (Quintus Horatius Flaccus; 65–8 B.C.). Together with Vergil and Ovid, one of the most significant and influential Latin poets. Writing in a variety of genres, he was a member of the group of poets patronized by the emperor Augustus.

Hyginus (2nd century A.D.?). Known, probably falsely, as the author of a handbook of mythology compiled from a variety of Greek sources.

Jove. Another name for Jupiter.

Juno. Roman equivalent of the Greek goddess Hera.

Jupiter. Chief god of the Romans. He became identified with the Greek god Zeus.

Laomedon. Legendary king of Troy.

Leda. Impregnated by Jupiter, who had taken on the form of a swan, she became the mother of Helen of Troy.

Livy (Titus Livius; 59 B.C.–A.D. 17). Author of a history of Rome from the origins of the city to the time of Augustus. Published in installments, the 142-chapter work won immediate acclaim.

Lucina. Name (meaning "goddess of light") for Juno in her capacity as goddess of childbirth.

Lucretius (Titus Lucretius Carus; ca. 94–55/51 B.C.). Latin author of the epic poem *On the Nature of the Universe*, which has become the principal source of information regarding Epicurean philosophy and its teachings.

Lydia. Kingdom in western Asia Minor.

Mars. Roman god of agriculture and war who became identified with the Greek god Ares.

Medusa. Mother of the winged horse Pegasus.

Melantho. Mother, by Neptune, of Delphus, from whom Delphi was thought to have derived its name.

Mercury. Roman equivalent of the Greek god Hermes.

Minerva. Roman goddess identified with the Greek goddess Athena.

Mnemosyne. Greek goddess of memory, who became the mother of the Muses, patron deities of the arts.

Moschus (act. ca. 150 B.C.). Greek writer of pastoral poetry. His few surviving works include a short epic poem entitled *Europa* that recounts the abduction of the Phoenician princess Europa by Zeus.

naiad. Variety of nymph presiding over springs, rivers, and lakes.

Nemesis. Goddess of retribution.

Neptune. Roman equivalent of the Greek god Poseidon.

Nonnos (act. 3rd quarter of 5th century A.D.?). Greek poet from the city of Panopolis (modern Akhmīm, Egypt). His epic poem *The Dionysiaca* centers on the life and exploits of the god Dionysus.

Oebalus. Legendary Spartan king and ancestor of Hyacinthus.

Ortygia. Island off the Sicilian coast at Syracuse.

Ovid (Publius Ovidius Naso; 43 B.C.–A.D. 17/18). Among the best known and highly acclaimed of Latin poets. His work includes the *Metamorphoses*, the epic poem that for centuries has been the primary source of Greek and Roman myth and legend.

Pactolus. River in Lydia.

Palici. Sons of Zeus and the Muse Thalia who were worshipped at the town of Palica in Sicily.

Pan. Greek patron god of flocks and herdsmen. He was associated with mountains, caves, and other remote wild places.

Panchaia. Fabled island rich in incense and gems thought to lie in the Indian Ocean.

Paphos. Along with Amathus, a town on the island of Cyprus that was a center of the worship of Venus.

Patara. City in Lycia sacred to Apollo.

Pausanias (ca. A.D. 115–180). Author of a description in Greek of mainland Greece based on his own travels. Cast as a travel guide, the work provides a wealth of information regarding many now-lost sites, monuments, and artworks as well as the customs and beliefs of the regions that he visited.

Persephone. Queen of the underworld and wife of Hades. Persephone, known to the Romans as Proserpina, was the daughter of the goddess Demeter.

Petronius (1st century A.D.). Author of the *Satyricon*, best known for its lively depiction of the gauche, nouveau-riche former slave Trimalchio and his outrageously elaborate banquet. The work's author is likely the same Petronius who was the "authority on elegance" in the court of the emperor Nero, and who was forced to commit suicide in A.D. 66.

Phocaea. Coastal city in Asia Minor that fell under Lydian control.

Phocaean murex. See *Phoenician dye*.

Phoebus. Another name for the god Apollo.

Phoenician dye. Precious red-purple dye extracted from the murex shell. Its chief producers were the seafaring people of Phoenicia who lived on the coast of what is now Lebanon.

Phrygia. Kingdom in the west-central part of Anatolia, in what is now Turkey.

Pindar (act. ca. 498–446 B.C.). Greek lyric poet known chiefly for his commemoration of victors at the Olympic and Pythian Games, which were held in a religious context at the sanctuaries of Olympia (sacred to Zeus) and Delphi (sacred to Apollo), respectively.

Plato (428/27–348/47 B.C.). Athenian philosopher and founder of the philosophical community or school that came to be called the Academy. Among Plato's many writings is *The Republic*, a discourse on the ideal state, which features Socrates (by whom Plato had been deeply influenced) as a character.

Pliny the Elder (Gaius Plinius Secundus; A.D. 23/24–79). Roman statesman, admiral, and scholar who was among the victims of Vesuvius's eruption. A prolific writer on topics that included grammar, oratory, military tactics, and biography, he is chiefly remembered for his extensive encyclopedic work on natural history, which encompasses topics including astronomy, botany, geology, horticulture, medicine, mineralogy, and zoology.

Plutarch (Lucius? Mestrius Plutarchus; ca. A.D. 45–125). Biographer and moral philosopher. His surviving works consist of a collection of treatises on morality, physics, literature, and other subjects as well as his biographies of eminent Greek and Roman political and military figures.

Pluto. Another Greek name for the god Hades, which was adopted by the Romans. The Romans also called him Dis.

Poseidon. Greek god of the sea, earthquakes, and horses. He competed unsuccessfully with Athena to become the patron deity of Athens. His Roman equivalent was Neptune.

Proserpina. Roman name for Persephone.

pygmies. In Minerva's tapestry, mythological dwarf inhabitants of Africa who were at war with the local population of cranes.

Sabaeans. Arabian tribe.

Saturn. Roman god of agriculture and fertility who became identified with the Greek god Cronus. He assaulted a nymph named Philyra, who subsequently gave birth to the centaur Chiron.

Schoeneus. Legendary Greek king of Boeotia and father of Atalanta.

Scythia. Region of central Eurasia whose nomadic inhabitants were renowned archers.

Semiramis. Wife of Ninus, a mythical king of Assyria, who assumed the crown upon his death. She was said to have been responsible for the formidable wall of brick that surrounded the city of Babylon.

Servius (Marius Servius Honoratus; act. ca. A.D. 400). Roman grammarian and commentator best known for his extensive commentary on the works of Vergil.

Soranus (act. ca. A.D. 98–138). Physician in Rome under the emperors Trajan and Hadrian. Having studied medicine in Alexandria, Egypt, he authored some twenty works in Greek on the history of medicine, medical terminology, and the practice of medicine.

Strabo (ca. 65 B.C.–A.D. 25). Historian and geographer. He is known primarily for his wide-ranging work in Greek on geography, inclusive of Spain, Gaul, Italy, the Balkans, Asia Minor, India, Egypt, North Africa, and more.

Stygian waters. See *Styx*.

Styx. River in the underworld.

Tartarus. Part of the underworld where the wicked suffer punishment. In the tale of Pluto and Persephone, Ovid uses it as a synonym for the underworld as a whole.

Tenedos. Island near Troy sacred to Apollo.

Theophrastus (ca. 371/70–288/86 B.C.). Greek philosopher who became the associate and successor of Aristotle. His numerous writings include works on metaphysics, physics, zoology, and physiology. Having produced the first systematic study of plants, he became known as the "father of botany." His botanical work was based on both personal observation and the reports of those who traveled with Alexander the Great on the latter's quest to conquer the vast Persian Empire and beyond.

Thrace. Region, with boundaries shifting over time, that extended roughly over what are now southeastern Bulgaria, northwestern Greece, and European Turkey.

Tmolus, Mount. In Lydia.

Varro (Marcus Terentius; 116–27 B.C.). Roman polymath and statesman. Described by the first-century A.D. rhetorician Quintilian as "the most learned of Romans" (*Inst.* 10.1.95), Varro reputedly authored some seventy-five works on diverse subjects, qualifying him as the most prolific of Latin authors, too. Only his treatise *On Agriculture*, a portion of his work *On the Latin Language*, and fragments of his poetic output survive.

Venus. Goddess of fertility and gardens identified by the Romans with Aphrodite.

Vergil (Publius Vergilius Maro; 70–19 B.C.). Illustrious author of the *Aeneid*, an epic poem recounting the founding of Rome and the origins of the Roman people. Vergil, who enjoyed the patronage of Augustus, was also the author of the *Eclogues*, a group of pastoral poems, and the *Georgics*, a didactic poem as much about agriculture as it is about the social and political concerns of the day.

Vitruvius (Marcus Vitruvius Pollio; ca. 80/70–15 B.C.). Roman architect and engineer who lived and worked during the regimes of Julius Caesar and the emperor Augustus. He is known chiefly for his *De architectura* (On architecture), the vastly influential and earliest surviving work on architecture and the art of building.

Zeus. King of the Greek gods. He was the god of weather and also the guarantor of civic rights, oaths, and the sacred bond between guest and host. He was known to the Romans as Jupiter.

SOURCES AND SUGGESTIONS FOR FURTHER READING

Ancient Authors

Aelian. *Aelian: Historical Miscellany.* Edited and translated by N. G. Wilson. Loeb Classical Library 486. Cambridge, Mass., 1997.

Apicius. *Apicius: A Critical Edition.* Edited and translated by Christopher Grocock and Sally Grainger. Devon, UK, 2006.

Apollodorus. *Apollodorus: The Library.* Edited and translated by James G. Frazer. 2 vols. Loeb Classical Library 121, 122. Cambridge, Mass., 1921.

Apollonius of Rhodes. *Apollonius Rhodius: The Argonautica.* Translated by R. C. Seaton. Loeb Classical Library 1. Cambridge, Mass., 1980.

Arnobius. *Arnobii adversus nationes libri vii.* Edited by August Reifferscheid. Vienna, 1875.

Athenaeus. *Athenaeus: The Deipnosophists.* Translated by Charles B. Gulick. 7 vols. Loeb Classical Library 204, 208, 224, 235, 274, 327, 345. Cambridge, Mass., 1961.

Cato. *On Agriculture.* In *Cato & Varro: De re rustica.* Translated by William D. Hooper and revised by Harrison B. Ash. Loeb Classical Library 283. Cambridge, Mass., 1979.

Celsus. *Celsus: De medicina.* Translated by Walter G. Spencer. 3 vols. Loeb Classical Library 292, 304, 336. Cambridge, Mass., 1935–38.

Cicero. *Cicero: Letters to Atticus.* Edited and translated by D. R. Shackleton Bailey. Vol. 1. Loeb Classical Library 5. Cambridge, Mass., 1998.

———. *Cicero's Letters to His Brother Quintus.* In *Cicero: Letters to Quintus and Brutus, Letter Fragments, Letter to Octavian, Invectives, Handbook of Electioneering.* Edited and translated by D. R. Shackleton Bailey. Loeb Classical Library 462. Cambridge, Mass., 2002.

Diodorus. *Diodorus Siculus: The Library of History.* Translated by C. H. Oldfather. Vol. 2. Loeb Classical Library 303. Cambridge, Mass., 1935.

Dioscorides. *De materia medica.* Translated by Tess A. Osbaldeston. Johannesburg, 2000.

Euripides. *Bacchanals.* In *Euripides: Bacchanals, Madness of Hercules, Children of Hercules, Phoenician Maidens, Suppliants.* Translated by Arthur S. Way. Loeb Classical Library 11. Cambridge, Mass., 1979.

Galen. *On the Properties of Foodstuffs.* Translated by Owen Powell. Cambridge, 2003.

Herodotus. *Herodotus: The Persian Wars.* Translated by Alfred D. Godley. Rev. ed. 4 vols. Loeb Classical Library 117–20. Cambridge, Mass., 1981–82.

Hesiod. *Theogony.* In *Hesiod, The Homeric Hymns, and Homerica.* Translated by Hugh G. Evelyn-White. Loeb Classical Library 57. Cambridge, Mass., 1982.

Hippocrates. *On Regimen.* In *Hippocrates: Volume IV.* Translated by W. H. S. Jones. Loeb Classical Library 150. Cambridge, Mass., 1923.

Homer [falsely attributed]. *Homeric Hymns.* In *Hesiod, The Homeric Hymns, and Homerica.* Translated by Hugh G. Evelyn-White. Loeb Classical Library 57. Cambridge, Mass., 1982.

Homer. *Homer: The Iliad.* Translated by A. T. Murray. 2 vols. Loeb Classical Library 170, 171. Cambridge, Mass., 1978.

———. *Homer: The Odyssey.* Translated by A. T. Murray. 2 vols. Loeb Classical Library 104, 105. Cambridge, Mass., 1984.

Horace. *Horace: The Odes and Epodes.* Translated by Charles E. Bennett. Loeb Classical Library 33. Cambridge, Mass., 1968.

———. *Horace: Satires, Epistles, and Ars poetica.* Translated by H. Rushton Fairclough. Loeb Classical Library 194. Cambridge, Mass., 1978.

Hyginus. *The Myths of Hyginus.* Edited and translated by Mary Grant. Lawrence, Kans., 1960.

Livy. *Livy: History of Rome.* Translated by B. O. Foster. Vol. 1. Loeb Classical Library 114. Cambridge, Mass., 1919.

———. *Livy: History of Rome.* Translated by B. O. Foster. Vol. 4. Loeb Classical Library 191. Cambridge, Mass., 1926.

Lucretius. *Lucretius: De rerum natura.* Translated by W. H. D. Rouse and revised by Martin F. Smith. 2nd ed. Loeb Classical Library 181. Cambridge, Mass., 1982.

Moschus. *The Poems of Moschus.* In *The Greek Bucolic Poets.* Translated by J. M. Edmonds. Loeb Classical

Library 28. Cambridge, Mass., 1977.
Nonnos. *Nonnos: Dionysiaca*. Translated by W. H. D. Rouse. 3 vols. Loeb Classical Library 344, 354, 356. Cambridge, Mass., 1984–85.
Ovid. *Ars amatoria*. In *Ovid: The Art of Love and Other Poems*. Translated by J. H. Mozley. 2nd rev. ed. Loeb Classical Library 232. Cambridge, Mass., 1979.
———. *De medicamina faciei*. In *Ovid: The Art of Love and Other Poems*. Translated by J. H. Mozley. 2nd rev. ed. Loeb Classical Library 232. Cambridge, Mass., 1979.
———. *Metamorphoses, Books 1–5*. Edited by William S. Anderson. Norman, Okla., 1997.
———. *Metamorphoses, Books 6–10*. Edited by William S. Anderson. Norman, Okla., 1972.
———. *Ovid: Fasti*. Translated by Sir James G. Frazer and revised by G. P. Goold. 2nd ed. Loeb Classical Library 253. Cambridge, Mass., 1989.
———. *Ovid: Tristia, Ex ponto*. Translated by Arthur L. Wheeler. Loeb Classical Library 151. Cambridge, Mass., 1939.
Pausanias. *Pausanias: Description of Greece*. Translated by W. H. S. Jones and H. A. Ormerod. 5 vols. Loeb Classical Library 93, 183, 272, 297, 298. Cambridge, Mass., 1918–35.
Petronius. *Satyricon*. In *Petronius: Satyricon; Seneca, Apocolocyntosis*. Translated by W. H. D. Rouse. Rev. ed. Loeb Classical Library 15. Cambridge, Mass., 1975.
Pindar. *Olympian Odes*. In *Pindar: Olympian Odes, Pythian Odes*. Edited and translated by William H. Race. Loeb Classical Library 56. Cambridge, Mass., 1997.
Plato. *Plato: The Republic*. Translated by Paul Shorey. 2 vols. Loeb Classical Library 237, 276. Cambridge, Mass., 1963.
Pliny the Elder. *The Natural History of Pliny*. Translated by John Bostock and Henry T. Riley. 6 vols. London, 1855.
Plutarch. *Alexander*. In *Plutarch: Lives, Demosthenes and Cicero, Alexander and Caesar*. Translated by Bernadotte Perrin. Loeb Classical Library 99. Cambridge, Mass., 1919.
Servius. *Servii grammatici qui feruntur in Vergilii carmina commentarii*. Edited by Georg Thilo and Hermann Hagen. 3 vols. Hildesheim, 1986.
Soranus. *Gynecology*. Translated by Oswei Temkin. Baltimore, 1956.
Strabo. *The Geography of Strabo*. Translated by Hans C. Hamilton and William Falconer. 3 vols. London, 1903.
Theophrastus. *Theophrastus: Enquiry into Plants*. Translated by Sir Arthur Hort. 2 vols. Loeb Classical Library 70, 79. Cambridge, Mass., 1916.
Varro. *On Agriculture*. In *Cato & Varro: De Re Rustica*. Translated by William D. Hooper and revised by Harrison B. Ash. Loeb Classical Library 283. Cambridge, Mass., 1979.
Vergil. *Georgics*. In *Virgil: Eclogues, Georgics, Aeneid I–VI*. Rev. ed. Translated by H. Rushton Fairclough. Loeb Classical Library 63. Cambridge, Mass., 1978.
Vitruvius. *Vitruvius: On Architecture*. Translated by Frank Granger. 2 vols. Loeb Classical Library 251, 280. Cambridge, Mass., 1931–34.

General Bibliography

Bailey, L. H. *The Standard Cyclopedia of Horticulture*. 2nd ed. 3 vols. New York, 1942.
Baumann, Hellmut. *The Greek Plant World in Myth, Art, and Literature*. Translated by William T. Stearn and Eldwyth Ruth Stearn. Portland, Ore., 1993.
Bergmann, Bettina. "Staging the Supernatural: Interior Gardens of Pompeian Houses." In *Pompeii and the Roman Villa: Art and Culture around the Bay of Naples*, edited by Carol Mattusch, 53–69. Exh. cat. Washington, D.C., National Gallery of Art, 2008.
Bernhardt, Peter. *Gods and Goddesses in the Garden: Greco-Roman Mythology and the Scientific Names of Plants*. New Brunswick, N.J., 2008.
Bowe, Patrick. *Gardens of the Roman World*. Los Angeles, 2004.
Carroll, Maureen, ed. *Earthly Paradises: Ancient Gardens in History and Archaeology*. Los Angeles, 2003.
Cartledge, Paul, ed. *Cambridge Illustrated History of Ancient Greece*. Cambridge, 1998.
Ciarallo, Annamaria. *Gardens of Pompeii*. Translated by Lori-Ann Touchette. Los Angeles, 2001.
Dalby, Andrew. *Dangerous Tastes: The Story of Spices*. Berkeley, 2000.
———. *Food in the Ancient World from A to Z*. London, 2003.
———. *Siren Feasts: A History of Food and Gastronomy in Greece*. London, 1996.
Detienne, Marcel. *The Gardens of Adonis: Spices in Greek Mythology*. Translated by Janet Lloyd. Atlantic Highlands, N.J., 1977.

Donato, Giuseppe, and Monique Seefried. *The Fragrant Past: Perfumes of Cleopatra and Julius Caesar*. Rome, 1989.

Dweck, Anthony C. "The Folklore of Narcissus." In *Narcissus and Daffodil: The Genus Narcissus*, edited by Gordon R. Hanks, 19–29. London, 2002.

Faraone, Christopher A. *Ancient Greek Love Magic*. Cambridge, Mass., 1999.

Farrar, Linda. *Ancient Roman Gardens*. Phoenix Mill, UK, 2000.

Fleming, Stuart J. *"Vinum": The Story of Roman Wine*. Glen Mills, Pa., 2001.

Frank, Tenney. *An Economic Survey of Ancient Rome*. Vol. 5, *Rome and Italy in the Empire*. Baltimore, 1940.

Garnsey, Peter. *Cities, Peasants, and Food in Classical Antiquity*. Cambridge, 1998.

———. *Food and Society in Classical Antiquity*. Cambridge, 1999.

Giesecke, Annette. *The Epic City: Urbanism, Utopia, and the Garden in Ancient Greece and Rome*. Cambridge, Mass., 2007.

———. "Outside In and Inside Out: Paradise in the Ancient Roman House." In *Earth Perfect? Nature, Utopia, and the Garden*, edited by Annette Giesecke and Naomi Jacobs, 118–25. London, 2012.

Gowers, Emily. *The Loaded Table: Representations of Food in Roman Literature*. Oxford, 1993.

Griffiths, Mark. *Index of Garden Plants*. Portland, Ore., 1994.

Hehn, Victor. *Cultivated Plants and Domesticated Animals in Their Migration from Asia to Europe: Historico-Linguistic Studies*. Revised by James P. Mallory. Amsterdam, 1976.

Heilmeyer, Marina. *Ancient Herbs*. Los Angeles, 2007.

Henderson, John. *The Roman Book of Gardening*. London, 2004.

Highet, Juliet. *Frankincense: Oman's Gift to the World*. Munich, 2006.

Huxley, Anthony, and William Taylor. *Flowers of Greece and the Aegean*. London, 1977.

Jashemski, Wilhelmina F. *The Gardens of Pompeii, Herculaneum, and the Villas Destroyed by Vesuvius*. 2 vols. New Rochelle, N.Y., 1979–93.

———. *A Pompeian Herbal: Ancient and Modern Medicinal Plants*. Austin, Tex., 1999.

Knox, Peter E., ed. *A Companion to Ovid*. Chichester, UK, 2009.

Lefkowitz, Mary R., and Maureen B. Fant, eds. *Women's Life in Greece and Rome*. London, 1982.

Maggiulli, Gigliola. *Incipiant Silvae cum Primum Surgere: Mondo Vegetale e Nomenclatura della Flora di Virgilio*. Rome, 1995.

McKay, A. G. *Houses, Villas, and Palaces in the Roman World*. Ithaca, N.Y., 1975.

Meiggs, Russell. *Trees and Timber in the Ancient Mediterranean World*. Oxford, 1982.

Miller, J. Innes. *The Spice Trade of the Roman Empire, 29 B.C. to A.D. 641*. Oxford, 1969.

Murr, Josef F. *Die Pflanzenwelt in der griechischen Mythologie*. Innsbruck, 1890.

Olson, Kelly. *Dress and the Roman Woman: Self-Presentation and Society*. London, 2008.

Peacock, David, and David Williams, eds. *Food for the Gods: New Light on the Ancient Incense Trade*. Oxford, 2007.

Phillips, Rod. *A Short History of Wine*. London, 2000.

Phillips, Roger, and Martyn Rix. *The Random House Book of Perennials*. 2 vols. New York, 1991.

Raven, J. E. *Plants and Plant Lore in Ancient Greece*. Oxford, 2000.

Scarborough, John. "The Pharmacology of Sacred Plants, Herbs, and Roots." In *Magika Hiera: Ancient Greek Magic and Religion*, edited by Christopher A. Faraone and Dirk Obbink, 138–74. Oxford, 1991.

Stewart, Susan. *Cosmetics & Perfumes in the Roman World*. Stroud, UK, 2007.

Syme, Ronald. *History in Ovid*. Oxford, 1978.

Thompson, Dorothy Burr, and Ralph E. Griswold. *Garden Lore of Ancient Athens*. Princeton, N.J., 1963.

Wallace-Hadrill, Andrew. *Houses and Society in Pompeii and Herculaneum*. Princeton, N.J., 1994.

Warrior, Valerie M. *Roman Religion*. New York, 2006.

White, K. D. *Roman Farming*. Ithaca, N.Y., 1970.

Willard, Pat. *Secrets of Saffron: The Vagabond Life of the World's Most Seductive Spice*. Boston, 1993.

Zohary, Daniel, and Maria Hopf. *Domestication of Plants in the Old World: The Origin and Spread of Cultivated Plants in West Asia, Europe, and the Nile Valley*. 3rd ed. Oxford, 2000.

Fourth printing

Published by the J. Paul Getty Museum, Los Angeles
Getty Publications
1200 Getty Center Drive, Suite 500
Los Angeles, CA 90049-1682
getty.edu/publications

Beatrice Hohenegger, *Editor*
Kurt Hauser, *Designer*
Elizabeth Kahn, *Production Coordinator*

Distributed in the United States and Canada by the University of Chicago Press

Distributed outside the United States and Canada by Yale University Press, London

Printed in China

Library of Congress Cataloging-in-Publication Data
Giesecke, Annette Lucia, author.
The mythology of plants : botanical lore from ancient Greece and Rome / Annette Giesecke.
pages cm
Includes bibliographical references.
ISBN 978-1-60606-321-7 (hardcover)
1. Plants—Mythology—Greece. 2. Plants—Mythology—Rome. 3. Botany—Greece—Folklore. 4. Botany—Rome—Folklore. 5. Plants in literature. 6. Mythology, Greek. 7. Mythology, Roman. I. Ovid, 43 B.C.-17 A.D. or 18 A.D. Metamorphoses. Selections. English. II. Title.
QK83.G54 2014
581—dc23
2013036033

Front Jacket: Alessandro Allori (Italian, 1535–1607), *The Abduction of Proserpine*, 1570 (detail, fig. 18)

Back Jacket: David Blair, *Morus nigra, Linn.*, London, 1880 (detail, fig. 42)

Pages 4–5: Camillo Miola (Italian, 1840–1919), *The Oracle*, 1880 (detail, fig. 14)

Page 6: David Blair, *Punica granatum, Linn.*, 1880 (detail, fig. 16)

Page 31: Frescoed wall with garden, detail of a branch with pomegranates. From House of Livia, Museo Nazionale Romano (Palazzo Massimo alle Terme), Rome, Italy.

Page 57: Frescoed wall with garden, detail of a branch with apples or quince. From House of Livia, Museo Nazionale Romano (Palazzo Massimo alle Terme), Rome, Italy.

MIX
Paper | Supporting responsible forestry
FSC® C008047
www.fsc.org

Page 91: Frescoed wall with garden and caged birds, detail of a branch of oak, from House of Livia, Museo Nazionale Romano (Palazzo Massimo alle Terme), Rome, Italy.

Page 101: Frescoed wall with garden, detail of a branch with apples or quince. From House of Livia, Museo Nazionale Romano (Palazzo Massimo alle Terme), Rome, Italy.

Page 115: Pine tree, flowers, and birds in garden, fresco, 20–10 B.C., Roman. From triclinium of House of Livia, Museo Nazionale Romano (Palazzo Massimo alle Terme), Rome, Italy

Page 116: Outer Peristyle Garden, Getty Villa, Malibu

Illustration Credits

Every effort has been made to contact the owners and photographers of objects reproduced here whose names do not appear in the captions or in the illustration credits listed below. Anyone having further information concerning copyright holders is asked to contact Getty Publications so this information can be included in future printings.

Figs. 1–7, 9, 25: © Annette Giesecke

Figs. 8, 10, 13–15, 17, 18, 21–23, 28, 30, 33, 34, 37, 39, 44, 45; pp. 4–5, p. 116: The J. Paul Getty Museum

Fig. 11: The Stapleton Collection / The Bridgeman Art Library

Figs. 12, 16, 27, 32, 36, 38, 42; p. 6: Courtesy Special Collections, University of Delaware Library, Newark, Delaware

Fig. 19: Los Angeles, Getty Research Institute (89-B10813)

Fig. 20: Museo Thyssen-Bornemisza / Scala / Art Resource, NY

Fig. 24: The LuEsther T. Mertz Library, NYBG / Art Resource, NY

Figs. 26, 35: © RMN-Grand Palais / Art Resource, NY

Fig. 29, 40: Courtesy The Winterthur Library: Printed Book and Periodical Collection

Fig. 31: © Ullstein Bild – Aisa

Fig. 41: Bibliothèque des Arts Décoratifs, Paris, France / Archives Charmet / The Bridgeman Art Library

Fig. 43: Bridgeman-Giraudon / Art Resource, NY

Fig. 46: Prado, Madrid, Spain / The Bridgeman Art Library

Pages 31, 57, 91, 101: Scala / Art Resource, NY. Photo: Luciano Romano

Page 115: Gianni Dagli Orti / The Art Archive at Art Resource, NY

Page 134: Map of Ancient Greece and the Mediterranean World by David L. Fuller, DLF Group